ASP
LEARNING
BY EXAMPLE

Robert B. Mellor
IT University of Copenhagen

A|B|F Content · 8536 SW St. Helens Drive, Suite D · Wilsonville, OR 97070 · www.abfcontent.com

President and Publisher	Jim Leisy (jimleisy@fbeedle.com)
Production	Stephanie Welch
	Tom Sumner
Manuscript Editor	Stephanie Welch
Cover Design	Ian Shadburne
Marketing	Christine Collier
Order Processing	Krista Brown

Library of Congress Cataloging-in-Publication Data

Mellor, Robert B.
 ASP : learning by example / Robert B. Mellor.
  p. cm.
 Includes index.
 ISBN 1-887902-68-6
  1. Active server pages. 2. Web sites--Design. 3. Web sites--Design--Problems, exercises, etc. I. Title.

TK5105.8885.A26 M45 2001
005.2'76--dc21

2001033978

A | B | F Content is an imprint of Franklin, Beedle & Associates, Incorporated.

TABLE OF CONTENTS

PREFACE

This book is intended for use in a short course focusing on ASP programming, as a supplement in a course on Web programming, or in a self-study program. Minimal experience with personal computers is assumed, principally the ability to do basic computer operations such as launch application programs, perform tasks with application programs, and access the Internet. Although a background in computer programming is helpful, it is not necessary.

This book contains 27 examples of ASP coding, each followed by a detailed explanation. Theory, tips, and new concepts are introduced along the way, in the body of the text as well as in the examples. You can download all code examples and files and get additional information from the publisher's Web site (**http:// www.abfcontent.com**).

Experience shows quite clearly that if you sit down at your PC and read/work through the book you will be able to do most ASP programming within a few days. Further explanations are found in the appendices, and a list of Web links is provided at the end of the book.

To execute ASP files you need access to a server with an ASP interpreter. The most commonly used one is Personal Web Server. However, Internet Information Server (IIS), Jigsaw, and WebSite Professional are also available. PWS is a small-scale version of IIS. PWS demands a browser of at least version 4.

The Author

Dr. Robert B. Mellor works at the IT University of Copenhagen. He has 14 years of teaching experience in several countries and is Examiner at many universities all over the world.

Symbols and Conventions

Text written in `Courier` represents code. There should not be breaks in ASP code when written in your HTML editor. However, in real life (in your editor program and in this book) it can be difficult to get everything on one line. The underscore character (_) is used (and interpreted by the machine) to indicate that the code lines are actually one line, despite the fact that there may be carriage returns in the line.

Disclaimer

This book is about Active Server Pages (ASP). Therefore, Structured Query Language (SQL), Microsoft Access, Personal Web Server (PWS), and VBScript are included out of necessity, but only in the degree needed to understand ASP. Interested readers are referred to texts specialized in those areas for further information on these subjects, as well as to this book's supporting material on the publisher's Web site (**http://www.abfcontent.com**).

DEVELOPMENT OF THE INTERNET AND THE NEED FOR INTEGRATION

"Never do anything a machine can do for you" is an old adage. It is not a call to be lazy, but rather a cry for efficiency. Human labor costs money, typically $2,000 a month. A new PC costs half that to buy and is written off over a period of typically three years (that is, the actual cost for a firm is zero), so why not let machines do the mundane, repetitive tasks and let humans get on with the interesting, expertise-demanding work? This realization has led to a revolution in all branches of human endeavor during the last 20 years. It also applies to the Internet.

Internet Web sites are divided into "generations" according to their level of sophistication. There are 3–6 generations, depending on whom you ask (I'm going to say 3). Quite simply, the early generations (1–2) are basically a "business card on the Web." It is improbable that anyone has ever sold anything using this type of Web site, but businesses are rarely aware that this level of Web site involves only expenses.

The middle generations (3–4) signify the stage where businesses are investing significantly in Web sites. They may have several sites; they may be paying a webmaster to put their catalogs on the Web; certainly someone is busy receiving a lot of emails from customers. To put it plainly, they are using the Internet just as they are using other advertising media (such as newspaper ads and direct mailing). This means extra marketing costs (because they haven't cut down on the other media, the Internet is an extra) plus a heavy investment in support personnel.

In the next generation, the Internet "moves in." Orders are no longer emailed to a secretary, but are programmed directly to the warehouse; catalogs are no longer printed, only printed out if needed; communication is over email and the intranet; the firm has gone over to electronic business and nobody is doing anything a machine can do. This total reorganization of a firm (sometimes called Business Process Re-engineering, or BPR) makes the organization very efficient.

Table 1: The generations of Web sites

Generation	Costs	Returns
Third	Large initial investment	High
Second	Extra personnel and advertising	Medium
First	Domain name, hosting, etc.	Nothing

It's clear that the higher you go up the generation ladder, the higher the degree of integration demanded. Figure 1 illustrates the enormous increase in demands regarding the degree of software integration (and therefore, software compatibility) when one jumps from the second to the third generation.

Figure 1: Integration in the jump from using the WWW as an advertising medium to having an e-business

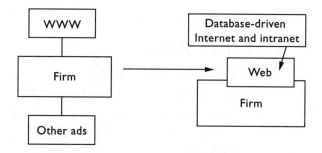

SOFTWARE COMPATIBILITY

There are many excellent programs "out there" that unfortunately rarely get used.
Let's look at a few of the major ones.

Table 2: Major programs

Program Area	Microsoft	Alternative
Browser	Internet Explorer	Netscape Navigator
Intranet server	NT4	Novell
Internet server	IIS	Unix/Apache
Back end	Office	Corel
Database	Access	Oracle
HTML editor	FrontPage	HomeSite, Dreamweaver, and others
Dynamic content	ASP	PHP3 and ColdFusion
	ISAPI	CGI/Perl
Email	Outlook	Eudora, GroupWise, and others
Software "glue" to stick it all together	Visual Basic	C++

I know many people in the IT branch who, if asked for their purely personal opinion, would say that more or less all of the programs listed under "Alternative" are better than the corresponding ones from Microsoft. However, if the owner of a business came along and asked them "I want a Web site that is fully back-end integrated, which software should I choose?" they would answer "Microsoft," because the Microsoft programs have a high degree of compatibility; the Microsoft programs "talk to each other."

When a customer orders something over the Internet, the payment goes one way (to the bank or the finance department); the order goes a different way, ending up at the warehouse; an email confirmation is sent back to the customer; the administration is notified; and the Web site is automatically updated. All the programs listed under "Alternative" are from different firms and, with a few honorable exceptions, are difficult to get to "talk to each other." Getting even a simple chain (like the one described above) to work can be a lengthy, frustrating, and therefore expensive process. Firm owners don't want that. They want a project that keeps to both the budget and the time schedule. Therefore, the head of the IT department will almost always recommend Microsoft.

ASP is the core of this style of integrated technology!

CLIENT-SIDE AND SERVER-SIDE SCRIPTING

The *de facto* standard for client-side scripting is JavaScript or some close derivative of JavaScript like JScript. In client-side scripting the requested file is saved to the browser's cache and is executed (or affects browser behavior in some way) from the local hard disk. Client-side scripting (with ActiveX, DHTML, CSS, Java applets, etc.) adds interest and effects to Web documents without increasing server loads.

Server-side scripting is more flexible, especially with respect to database access. Scripts executed on the server usually generate customized replies for the client. For example, if you wanted to fly from London to Bangkok on the 4th of July, the database could be queried and the dynamically-generated HTML sent back to the client. You cannot do that with client-side scripting!

WHAT IS ASP?

When a Web document is written in pure HTML, we call it "flat." Such documents, when viewed in a browser, are static; that is, they always have the same, unchanging content. Web sites made purely with HTML technology are the dinosaurs of the Web world—huge, inflexible, and doomed to extinction. Imagine a Web site where you can buy shoes. The first Web document, upon being viewed by Ted, says "Hi Ted" and shows all the shoes in size 9 (Ted's shoe size) at a price of $40. The very same document, upon being viewed by Tony, says "Hi Tony" and shows the shoes in Tony's size (size 10), but the price is now only $36, because Tony is a preferred customer and gets a 10% discount. This is what we call "dynamic content." Imagine two Web sites, one flat and one dynamic. Which one is the more interesting and the more user-friendly, the one that is best in attracting (and retaining) the most customers?

One characteristic of dynamic Web documents is that they change their content every time they are viewed. Examples are sites for the weather, the latest news, or stock prices (often updated several times every minute). Every time the user (often called the "client") refreshes the browser, the server provides an updated version. Active Server Pages (ASP) is an excellent tool for making such Web sites. With ASP, Internet programmers can combine standard HTML elements (tables, text, links, and so on) with server-side scripting (databases, date/time functions, customization according to logon, and so on). This allows the programmer to make Web documents that are generated dynamically every time they are requested.

The process starts when the client requests an ASP document from the server. The server localizes the file and executes the script that the file contains. The document is then sent to the client as a normal HTML-coded document. It is important to remember that the final document sent to the client contains no ASP code, because this has already been executed by the server. Programmers can execute all their scripts on the server (server-side scripting) and thus completely avoid client-side scripting. This in turn means that the site can use advanced Web-design techniques and can still successfully show in old browsers, which normally would not be capable of showing advanced design features.

A popular misconception is that ASP is a programming language. This is wrong; ASP is not a programming language. On one hand, ASP is a process that can be programmed in a variety of languages (e.g., JScript or VBScript). On the other hand, it is also simply a file extension (.asp) that tells certain (but not all) server types how to interpret file content.

Figure 2: What happens with an ASP file?

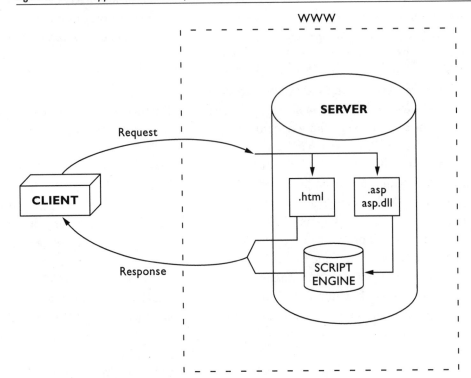

Figure 2 shows that the client can request either HTML or ASP (this is simply according to the extension on the file name—either .html or .asp). If the request is for HTML, then the response is to add the requested information to the HTML response stream flowing back to the client. If the request is for ASP, then the file asp.dll is used to find out what kind of scripts are needed. The .dll extension stands for Dynamic

Link Library, and asp.dll is an ActiveX component that reads the file (parses) from top to bottom and is able to "farm out" the various codes to the appropriate script engines (JScript, VBScript, and so on) to be executed. The server then puts the results of these operations back together and adds the dynamically-generated HTML back into the client-bound HTML stream.

PERSONAL WEB SERVER 4

In order to execute ASP files you must have access to a server with an ASP interpreter (asp.dll or similar). Usually this is Personal Web Server 4.0 (PWS4). However, there are others, for example Microsoft's Internet Information Server (IIS), Jigsaw, and O'Reilly's WebSite Professional. PWS is a small-scale version of IIS. PWS (but not ASP) demands a browser of at least version 4. Be aware that if you open a random ASP file (for example, on your desktop) in your browser, it will not execute. This is because you have a Windows path (you can recognize this by the backslash sign, \ ) and not an HTTP path (recognizable by the slash sign, /). To execute ASP files you must have a server running and be in the server's HTTP environment. To use PWS all files must be placed in the PWS root or in subdirectories under the PWS root, C:\Inetpub\wwwroot. Open your browser and type **http://localhost/file_name.asp** in the address line. Figure 3 shows PWS Manager after you have opened it (either from the start line or by choosing it under Programs).

Figure 3: Personal Web Manager

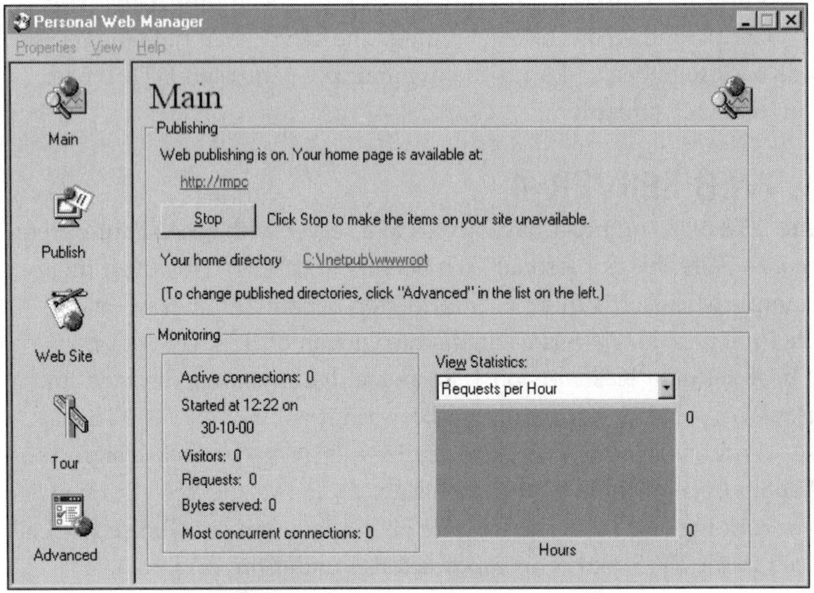

To show the content of the root directory C:\Inetpub\wwwroot in your browser, make sure to check "Allow Directory Browsing" (under "Advanced" in Personal Web Manager).

Figure 4: Advanced Options in Personal Web Manager

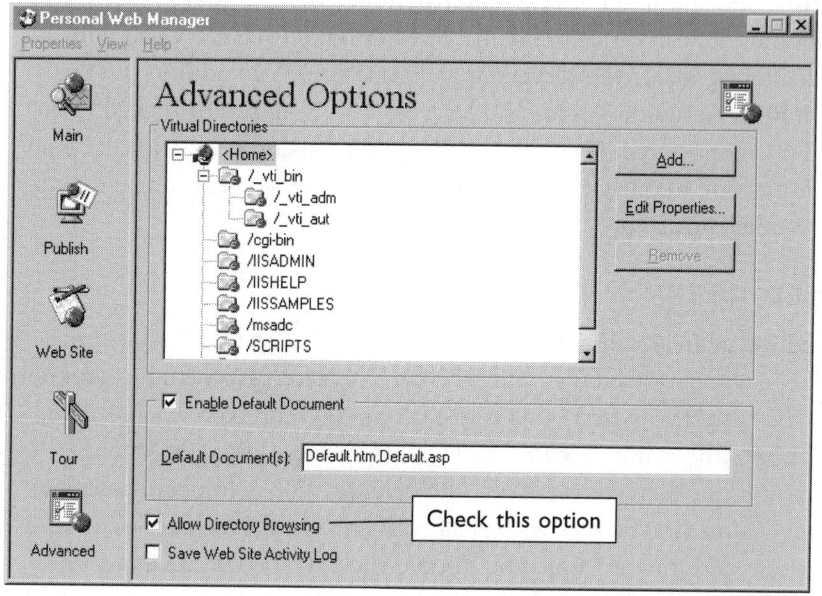

You can also view files that other PCs in your local area network (LAN) have on their servers by typing the name of their PC in the address line. Note that "localhost" means the server on your PC. You may, however, also use your PC's name. My PC is called rmpc (see Figure 3), thus I can type **http://rmpc/file_name.asp** in my browser address field, or even **http://127.0.0.1/file_name.asp** because 127.0.0.1 is the loopback default IP address for PWS installations. If I have a coworker in my LAN who has a PC called PC2, then I can look at their results by typing **http://PC2/file_name.asp** in my browser address field.

PWS first came out with Windows 98, and it can be obtained from **www.microsoft.com**. You should be aware that installing PWS on older systems (like ones running Windows 95) can cause problems. Furthermore, PWS can clash with older programs, including local Web servers (e.g., FrontPage97). In addition to the PWS software, the PWS Network Service and Microsoft TCP/IP protocol need to be correctly installed and configured. If you have NT4 and are using IIS there will be no major problems, but again, updates (server packs) may be needed and can be downloaded from **www.microsoft.com**.

EDITING ASP FILES

ASP files can be edited in an ASCII editor, like Notepad, or in the HTML editor of your choice. It can be a good idea to associate the file extension .asp with the program you wish to use. The easiest way to do this is to click on the **Start** icon, choose **Run**, and type **WINFILE** into the resulting command box. In the resulting File Manager box, highlight any ASP file, then choose **Associate** from the File menu, and associate the program you wish to edit ASP files with (you may have to choose **Browse** to find it). Close File Manager and the next time you double-click on an ASP file in a Windows environment, it will open in your favorite editor program.

Example A: A Simple ASP Script

In this example we choose a standard server-side script and write the result to the client (the browser).

1. Open your HTML editor and type the following:

```
<%@ Language=VBScript%>
<HTML>
```

```
<HEAD><TITLE>Starting ASP</TITLE></HEAD>
<BODY>
<%
Response.Write "I am your first ASP<BR>"
Response.Write Time
'Comments are written preceded by a single quotation mark ...
%>
</BODY>
</HTML>
```

2. Save the document as C:\inetpub\wwwroot\start.asp.

3. Start your browser and type **http://localhost/start.asp** in the address field.

Explanation

Which language is being used?

```
<%@ Language=VBScript%>
```

This line tells the server that the script is written in VBScript. This is often left out, because the default script language on PWS and IIS servers is VBScript (a script evolved from Visual Basic). However, later we will see some examples in JScript (Microsoft's adaptation of JavaScript). ASP is mostly written in VBScript, and therefore we will also use VBScript here. If you do include the language information, then it must always be in the first line, otherwise an error response is provoked.

The tag <% tells the server that ASP code is beginning, and %> tells the server that now the coding portion is over.

```
Response.Write "I am your first ASP<BR>"
```

Response is an object. Write is one of its methods, and it results in everything between the quotation marks being written to the client (the browser). The quotation marks are not interpreted, so **I am your first ASP
** is what appears in the HTML code. Note that we have mixed ASP and HTML. All the browser shows is

> I am your first ASP

```
Response.Write Time
```

Here again we use the Response object and its method Write. However, instead of using quotation marks and thus writing literally the concrete text, we call the standard function Time. This takes the time from the server's internal clock and writes it to the document. Try now to refresh your browser—you see the time is updated. To see the difference between calling a function and simply writing, return to your HTML editor and put Time in quotation marks (like "Time"). Refresh your browser.

```
'Comments are written preceded by a single quotation mark ...
```

This line starts with a single quotation mark. Lines written like this are not executed, because they are not even seen by the server. This is useful if you want to leave comments and guidelines for yourself or others to read at a later date. Note that this method only works within <% %> fields. Otherwise you have to use the JavaScript (/ / for single lines or /* */ for many lines) or HTML (<!-- and -->) method of hiding comments, according to your document.

SAVING AND VIEWING

The file was saved in the directory C:\inetpub\wwwroot\ and was called start.asp. When it was opened by typing **http://localhost/start.asp** in the browser address field, the code was executed by the server and the resulting pure HTML was sent to the browser. If you look at the browser source you will see only

```
<HTML>
<HEAD><TITLE>Starting ASP</TITLE></HEAD>
```

```
<BODY>
I am your first ASP<BR>09:34:12
</BODY>
</HTML>
```

Example B: Execution Order in ASP Scripts

In this example we will look at the execution order (or how asp.dll works), see an example of JScript, plus use a shortcut for Response.Write.

1. Open your editor and type the following:

```
<%@ Language=VBScript %>
<HTML>
<HEAD></HEAD>
<BODY>
<%
Dim var_two
Dim var_ten
var_two = "Declared variable string Two "
var_ten = 10
'note that var_two is a string text defined using quotation
'marks whereas var_ten as an integer is defined without
'quotation marks
%>
<BR>One in HTML<BR>
<%= var_two %> <BR>
Three in HTML<P>
<script language=VBScript runat=server>
Response.Write "Four VBScript runat server"
</script>
```

```
Five in HTML<BR>
<%= "Six written inline with shortcut" %><BR>
<script language=JScript runat=server>
Response.Write ("Seven JScript runat server");
</script>
<P>Eight in HTML<BR>
Nine in HTML<BR>
<%= var_ten %><BR>
</BODY>
</HTML>
```

2. Save the document as C:\inetpub\wwwroot\xorder.asp.

3. Start your browser and type **http://localhost/xorder.asp** in the address field.

4. View the source code.

Explanation

Two variables are defined in a code block. The notation Dim (for "dimension") is used to declare that the variables exist; then their values are assigned. In this case they are a string (text) value and an integer (numerical) value:

```
<%
Dim var_two
Dim var_ten
var_two = "Declared variable string Two "
var_ten = 10
```

The shortcut tags <%= and %> are then used instead of Response.Write to write the value (in this case text) of the variable.

```
<BR>One in HTML<BR>
<%= var_two %> <BR>
Three in HTML<P>
```

Shortcuts are written on the same line and inside <% and %>. They are used to write ASP values within larger blocks of HTML code. This method is called "inline." They can also be used to write literal text (or integers), in which case the value is cited in quotation marks:

```
<%= "Six written inline with shortcut" %>
```

In two places script blocks are used

```
<script language=Script runat=server>
Response.Write ""
</script>
```

to declare the scripting language (in this example either VBScript or JScript) and that it should be executed at the server. In both cases the Response.Write method is used. Note that JScript, as all JavaScript versions, needs the function parentheses and the terminating semicolon (;).

The document's HTML source should look like this:

```
Seven JScript runat server
<HTML>
<HEAD></HEAD>
<BODY>
<BR>One in HTML<BR>
Declared variable string Two   <BR>
```

```
Three in HTML<P>
Five in HTML<BR>
Six written inline with shortcut<BR>
<P>Eight in HTML<BR>
Nine in HTML<BR>
10<BR>
</BODY>
</HTML>
Four VBScript runat server
```

As you see, the file was parsed (read) by asp.dll and those scripts that were not declared as scripts were sent to the appropriate script engine for execution first. In this case the declared script was in VBScript; the script that was not default was in JScript. After that the HTML and inline code were executed, and lastly, the remaining default script was sent to the script engine and executed. You can test this by simply changing the script language in <%@ Language=VBScript %> to JScript (remember to change the comment marks, if you have them, to //). In that case the source would look like

```
Four VBScript runat server
<HTML>
<HEAD></HEAD>
<BODY>
<BR>One in HTML<BR>
Declared variable string Two   <BR>
Three in HTML<P>
Five in HTML<BR>
```

```
Six written inline with shortcut<BR>
<P>Eight in HTML<BR>
Nine in HTML<BR>
10<BR>
</BODY>
</HTML>
Seven JScript runat server
```

As you see, this case is exactly the same as before, in that the nondeclared script (now VBScript) was executed first, the declared script last, and the HTML and the inline code in between.

CONDITIONAL EXPRESSIONS

What variables are and how they can be manipulated will be described shortly. What's important is that once we have something (a variable), we can compare it to something else and take an action based upon whether the variable is the same as our criterion or not, i.e., if it satisfies a condition.

Example C: A Dynamic ASP Script

In this example we will use a standard server function called Hour (which is similar to the Time function we used in Example A) to get the present time. This variable is compared to defined integers as a starting point for branching based on conditions. We will go into branching later. We also see that ASP files do not need to begin with <HTML>.

1. Open your HTML editor and type the following:

```
<% If Hour(Now) >= 6 And Hour(Now) <= 18 Then %>

<HTML>
```

```
<HEAD>
<TITLE>Daytime</TITLE>
</HEAD>
<BODY BGCOLOR="#FFFFFF" TEXT="#000000">
<B>Day</B>
</BODY>
</HTML>

<% Else %>

<HTML>
<HEAD>
<TITLE>Nighttime</TITLE>
</HEAD>
<BODY BGCOLOR="#000000" TEXT="#FFFFFF">
<B>Night</B>
</BODY>
</HTML>

<% End If %>
```

2. Save the document as C:\inetpub\wwwroot\dynamic.asp.

3. Start your browser and type **http://localhost/dynamic.asp** in the address field.

4. Test the script by double-clicking on the time on the Start menu bar and changing the clock on your PC.

Explanation

```
<% If Hour(Now) >= 6 And Hour(Now) <= 18 Then %>
```

This is the condition. If the value of Hour returned from the server is larger than or equal to 6 and smaller than or equal to 18 then the first HTML document is returned.

Otherwise (Else) a second document is returned. Note that both HTML documents are written inside one ASP file.

We will come to If/Else branching statements later. For now just note the essential structure: IF – THEN – END IF. The structure of the branching statement rests upon a Boolean assumption; that is, whether something is true or false. It can have various structures: IF THEN or SELECT CASE. We will go into this later.

CONCATENATION

Example D: Concatenated Variables in Strings

1. Open your HTML editor and type in the following:

```
<%@ Language=VBScript%>
<HTML>
<HEAD>
<TITLE></TITLE>
</HEAD>
<BODY>
<%
Dim firstname, lastname
firstname = "John"
lastname = "Smith"
Response.Write "Hello " & firstname & " " & lastname & ".<BR>"
'note that the line above cannot be broken
%>
</BODY>
</HTML>
```

2. Save the document as C:\inetpub\wwwroot\concat.asp.

3. Start your browser and type **http://localhost/concat.asp** in the address field.

Explanation

Note that the variables have been declared as concatenated. It saves time, when declaring many variables, to dimension them on one line, separated by commas (,). Response.Write first writes **Hello**. Note carefully the space immediately after the word Hello. The contents (text values) of the two variables come next, added by means of an ampersand (&). (Not a + sign!) In order to separate them with a space we have to include " " before we concatenate the second variable using `& lastname`. Lastly we concatenate again (using &) to write the specified HTML code. Variable names should contain only English (ASCII) letters; don't use an umlaut, a circumflex, and so on.

VARIABLES

Example E: Writing Variables to HTML Code and Using Integer (Whole Number) Variables

1. Open your HTML editor and type the following:

```
<%@ Language=VBScript%>
<%
firstname = "John"
lastname = "Smith"
shade = "lightcyan"
X = "Starting ASP"
headline = 1
%>
<HTML><HEAD>
<TITLE><%=X%></TITLE>
</HEAD>
<BODY bgcolor=<%=shade%>>
```

```
<H<%=headline%>>Hello there!
</H<%=headline%>>
Your name is:
<%
Response.Write firstname & " " & lastname
%>
</BODY>
</HTML>
```

2. Save the document as C:\inetpub\wwwroot\variable.asp.

3. Start your browser and type **http://localhost/variable.asp** in the address field.

Explanation

Notice there's no Dim. In ASP you don't need to declare variables, but it is a good idea (see the "Debugging" section). Furthermore, in ASP variables are principally typeless; you cannot *a priori* define what type they should be. (Remember in Visual Basic you can `Dim variablename as Integer` or whatever—you cannot do that in ASP.) However, X was defined here as a string variable because it was defined `X = "Starting ASP"` as text in quotation marks. Conversely, headline was defined as an integer: `headline = 1`. We can find out what kind of variable we have using the standard function varType:

```
Response.Write varType(headline)
Response.Write varType(x)
```

Sometimes we have to force variables to change their type. This is important when we have to do operations on variables; for example, addition. In the following code we have two variables as strings and as integers:

As strings	As integers
One="1"	One=1
Two="2"	Two=2
Response.write one + two	Response.write one + two
The result of the addition is 12	The result of the addition is 3

So you can see that it would be annoying if we had to calculate a total price and one of the variables we had to use had acquired the type string! In the next section we see what types variables can have and how to change their type.

Table 3: Types of variables

Name	Value	Description
Empty	0	Undefined
Null	1	Contains no data
Integer	2	Whole number between -32,768 and +32,767
Long	3	Whole number between -2,147,483,648 and +2,147,483,647
Single	4	Decimal number
Double	5	Decimal number
Currency	6	Currency
Date	7	Date
String	8	Text
Object	9	Object

Name	Value	Description *(continued)*
Error	10	Error
Boolean	11	True or false
Byte	17	Whole number between 0 and 255
Array	8.192	Table

Note that the entries under Value are the numbers varType() returns.

Table 4: Types of operators

Operator	Description
*	Multiplication
/	Division
Mod	Modulo (remainder after division)
+	Addition
-	Subtraction
&	Concatenation
<	Less than
<=	Less than or equal to
>	Greater than
>=	Greater than or equal to
=	Equal to
<>	Not equal to

And	Logical and
Or	Logical or
Not	Logical not

STARTING FORMS

Example F: Writing Information into a Form Field, Recovering It Again with Request.Form, and Printing It to the Browser with Response.Write

1. Open your HTML editor and type the following:

```
<%@ Language=VBScript%>
<HTML>
<HEAD></HEAD>
<BODY>

<FORM METHOD="POST">
<INPUT TYPE="TEXT" NAME="informationfield">
<INPUT TYPE="SUBMIT">
</FORM>

<%
strinformationfield = Request.Form("informationfield")
Response.Write strinformationfield
%>
</BODY>
</HTML>
```

2. Save the document as C:\inetpub\wwwroot\startform.asp.

3. Start your browser and type **http://localhost/startform.asp** in the address field.

Explanation

Of the two methods ASP has of transmitting information, forms are the most prevalent. Here we have an input (a text field) whose name is informationfield and whose value is what one wishes to write in the field. Notice that the variable with the name informationfield is already at this point defined as string (i.e., text). The variable is transmitted with METHOD="POST". This information is recovered using the request object. In this case we define a new variable—strinformationfield—and put its value equal to that of Request.Form("informationfield"), or the value informationfield has in the form. After this we can simply see what that value is using the response object.

THE ASP OBJECT MODEL

In this book we will not be exploring the object model much. We are already aquainted with the two most common objects—Response and Request. They are in all seven objects in the Object Model Structure.

Table 5: The object model structure

Object	Description
Response	This controls how information is sent back to the client, including the following: 1. insert data into the returned page 2. create cookies 3. redirect the client 4. send the created page bit by bit or wait until the whole page is made 5. control the page's properties (such as headers)

Request	This object is responsible for packaging the data an ASP application needs, including the following: 1. values in a form element (Request.Form) 2. value pairs in a URL (Request.QueryString) 3. getting (and showing) server variables 4. handling and collecting cookies 5. collecting any security certificates
Server	Server objects are abstractions of the server's properties and methods. For example, they set the time a script can run before an error is registered, convert strings to HTML or a URL, create ActiveX components like CreateObject, and change the course of execution by changing pages using Transfer and Execute.
Application	Application is used to store data that is accessible for all clients in an application.
Session	Session is used to store data about one client throughout that client's session.
ObjectContext	This is related to transactions and transaction management; for example, if two clients were updating a database at the same time, allowing one to proceed and postponing the other.
ASPError	The details of errors generated by asp.dll are stored in the ASPError object and accessed using Server.GetLastError.

More information can be found in the appendix.

BRANCHING

Branching is a technique used to split up responses according the content of the data. Comparisons and branching mean that whole blocks of code can be executed if a certain condition is fulfilled, or a whole different block is executed if the condition is not met. There are two methods, which are similar but are often used in different situations.

IF and IF ELSE	SELECT CASE

1. Simple If: This simple branch tests if one criterion is fulfilled.
If hour(now) = 1 Then
write what has to be done
End If
 	
2. If/Else: This tests if a criterion is fulfilled, and provides a "catch all" if it is not.
If hour(now) = 1 Then
write what has to be done
Else
write something else
End If
 	
3. If/Elseif: This allows several criteria to be repeatedly tested.
If hour(now) = 1 Then
write what has to be done
Elseif hour(now) = 2
do something too
End If
	Select case true
	case age < 18
	write you are a minor
	case age >= 18
	write you are the right age
	case age > 65
	write you are a senior citizen
	End select
	
	Note the use of "true" in Select case true. Either "true" or the name of the variable being tested must be given.

4. If/Elseif/Else: A combination of methods 2 and 3, allowing several criteria to be repeatedly tested as well as providing a "catch all" if none are fulfilled.
 	
If hour(now) = 1 Then
write what has to be done
Elseif hour(now) = 2
do something too
Else
write something else
End If
 	
Note that each and every If statement always ends with End If.	

Use if you want to look for one or two specific criteria amongst an unspecified number of possibilities and have a "catch all" in case none of them are true.	Use if you have a known number of possibilities, for example input from a select list.

Let us first see simple branching in action. Later we will see that IF and SELECT can easily be combined.

Example G: Using Nested IF Statements (One inside the Other) with AND to Check if Several Criteria Are True

1. Open your HTML editor and type the following:

```
<%@ Language=VBScript %>
<HTML>
<BODY>
<H2>Write your age</H2>
<FORM METHOD="POST">
<INPUT TYPE="TEXT" NAME="age">
<INPUT TYPE="SUBMIT">
</FORM>

<%
clientage = Request.Form("age")
If clientage <> "" Then
If clientage < 18 Then
Response.Write "You are too young!"
Elseif clientage >= 18 and clientage < 65 Then
Response.Write "You are the right age"
Else
Response.Write "You can join our senior citizens club!"
End If
Else
Response.Write "You have not written anything"
End If
%>

</BODY>
</HTML>
```

2. Save the document as C:\inetpub\wwwroot\branch.asp.

3. Start your browser and type **http://localhost/branch.asp** in the address field.

Explanation

In this example the client's input (the value of the variable age) is set to the client's age (the variable clientage). The first IF statement If clientage <> "" Then checks if the variable has a content, that is, if it is different from empty. After that comes a simple IF statement:

```
If clientage < 18 Then
Response.Write "You are too young!"
...
End If
```

Note the less-than operator, <. Other operators can be used here (see Table 4 above). These operators can be combined using AND (as well as OR or NOT), as above, for example:

```
Elseif clientage >= 18 and clientage < 65 Then
Response.Write "You are the right age"
```

The two IF statements are then each closed, that is, there are two END IFs. The "inner" of the nested IFs is closed first, after which the ELSE belonging to the first IF is written.

Please note at this point that it is a good idea to set a new variable (in the above example, called "clientage"), but it is not essential. Look at the following (note the use of OR in the IF statement, and the use of underscore (_) to join lines because these cannot be broken in ASP).

```
If Request.Form("variablename") = "x" or _
Request.Form("variablename") = "y" Then
Response.Write "X is as good as Y"
End If
```

Using OR saves time in writing what would otherwise be:

```
If variablename = "y" Then
If variablename = "y" Then
Response.Write "X is as good as Y"
End If
End If
```

Example H: Mixing IF and SELECT

SELECT CASE is very similar to IF. However, you have to specify which element is being compared and set each condition for that element.

1. Open your HTML editor and type the following:

```
<%@ Language=VBScript %>
<HTML>
<BODY>
<H2>Write your password</H2>
<FORM METHOD="POST">
<INPUT TYPE="TEXT" NAME="password">
<INPUT TYPE="SUBMIT">
</FORM>

<%
code = Request.Form("password")

If code <> "" Then
Select Case code
Case "member"
Response.Write "Welcome member, make yourself at home"
Case "guest"
```

```
Response.Write "Welcome guest, you have fewer rights _
than members have"
Case Else
Response.Write "Go away, we only accept members and guests"
End Select
End If
%>

</BODY>
</HTML>
```

2. Save the document as C:\inetpub\wwwroot\select.asp.

3. Start your browser and type **http://localhost/select.asp** in the address field.

4. Try it out with "guest," "member," or anything else as password.

   Notice here the use of Case Else as a "catch all" in case all of the other cases are false. AND, OR and NOT can be used in SELECT just as in IF, like this:

```
Case clientage >= 18 and clientage < 65
Response.Write "Welcome"
End Select
```

   SELECT can also be used for checking nonsequential values, as in the following example:

```
Select Case totalPrice
Case 0, 10, 30
Response.Write "Cheap"
Case 40, 50
Response.Write "Expensive"
End Select
```

ITERATING AND LOOPING

Iterating and looping are used when a certain piece of code has to be reiterated or repeatedly executed several times. As with branching, there are two methods that are similar but often used in different situations. These are FOR NEXT and DO LOOP.

FOR NEXT	DO LOOP
There are actually two types of FOR iterating: FOR NEXT and FOR EACH. The latter will be described later in connection with collections.	There are two types of DO LOOP: DO WHILE and DO UNTIL.

FOR NEXT:

```
For variable = startvalue To finishingvalue
the code to be executed
Next
```

For example:

```
For x = 1 To 5 Step 1
Response.Write "X is: " & x & "<BR>"
Next
```

displays the following in your browser:

X is: 1
X is: 2
X is: 3
X is: 4
X is: 5

DO LOOP:

```
Do Until condition
the code to be executed
Loop
Do While condition
the code to be executed
Loop
```

DO UNTIL will be executed again and again until the condition is fulfilled. For example:

```
Do Until x = 10
Response.Write "Do Until: " & x & "<BR>"
x = x + 1
Loop
```

DO WHILE is used the opposite way, in that looping is performed while the condition is true. For example:

	Do While x < 10 Response.Write "Do While: " & x & " " x = x + 1 Loop
FOR NEXT is used to perform a small or known number of repeats.	DO LOOP is used when a large or unknown number of repeats are to be performed. Remember to double-check that the condition can be reached, because everyone makes infinite loops sometime in her or his career!

Iterating and looping can also be nested, just as in branching. *Note:* Occasionally a shorthand syntax can be used, consisting of While and WhileEnd (Wend):

```
While condition
the code to be executed
Wend
```

Example 1: Using FOR NEXT to Make a Variable with Changing Value and Insert It into HTML

1. Open your HTML editor and type the following:

```
<%@ Language=VBScript %>
<HTML>
<BODY>

<%
For x = 1 To 6 Step 1
Response.Write "<h" & x & ">Header Size " & x & "</h" & x & ">"
Next
```

```
For x = 6 To 1 Step - 1
Response.Write "<h" & x & ">Header Size " & x & "</h" & x & ">"
Next
%>

</BODY>
</HTML>
```

2. Save the document as C:\inetpub\wwwroot\iterating1.asp.

3. Start your browser and type **http://localhost/iterating1.asp** in the address field.

   Note that Step can be positive or negative (using a minus sign, −).

   As was said before, For Each can be used to repeat an event or method for each element in a collection. Collections can be variables the server is set up with or the client has stored in an application or session. The syntax for For Each is

   For Each element In collection
   the code to be executed
   Next

Example J: Writing All the Elements in the Collection ServerVariables

1. Open your HTML editor and type the following:

```
<%@ Language=VBscript%>
<HTML>
<BODY>

<%
For Each item In Request.ServerVariables
Response.Write "<P>" & item & " = " & _
```

```
Request.ServerVariables(item)
Next
%>

</BODY>
</HTML>
```

2. Save the document as C:\inetpub\wwwroot\iterating2.asp.

3. Start your browser and type **http://localhost/iterating2.asp** in the address field.

Explanation

This script looks sequentially at each variable in the collection. While it is examining an element, that element is called "item," which is then written to the browser. Then Next simply makes the script look at the next variable, call that "item," and write that too. Next repeats this again and again until there are no more variables in the collection. This means that you do not have to know how many variables there are in the collection, which can be an advantage.

VALIDATING A FORM SUBMISSION

Example K: Variables Declared Using Dim and Option Explicit and Used to Check the Content of a Text String

1. Open your HTML editor and type the following:

```
<%@ Language=VBScript%>
<% Option Explicit %>
<HTML>
<HEAD></HEAD>
```

```
<BODY>
<FORM METHOD="POST">
<INPUT TYPE="TEXT" NAME="email">
<INPUT TYPE="SUBMIT">
</FORM>

<%
Dim Address
Address = Request.Form("email")
If inStr(Address, "@") and inStr(address, ".") > 0 Then
Response.Write "OK"
Else
Response.Write "You have not written a proper email address"
End If
%>
</BODY>
</HTML>
```

2. Save the document as C:\inetpub\wwwroot\valid.asp.

3. Start your browser and type **http://localhost/valid.asp** in the address field.

Explanation

When <% Option Explicit %> is used, all variables must be declared. The advantage of this is that any typing errors will automatically pop up as errors in variable definition. As said before, many variables can be declared at one time by simply putting them all on the same line, separated by commas.

```
If inStr(Address, "@") and inStr(address, ".") > 0 Then
Response.Write "OK"
```

InStr() is a function searching for a string in a string. A list of string functions is given in the appendix. Here inStr looks first for an @ and then for a dot (.) in the variable called address. InStr returns the letter number where the character is found, e.g., inStr("Active", "t") returns the value 3. Obviously, if the character is present, its value is greater than 0.

Clearly, in the above example, typing simply "@." returns a valid email address. Therefore, one can make the check a little more rigorous using

```
If inStr(Address, "@") > 2 and inStr(address, ".") > 5 Then
```

But, of course, it is never possible to check if an email address is really correct (and belongs to that person). Checking text box input can be harder, because one cannot check for special characters.

One therefore has to check to see if the returned string has a content. There are two common methods of doing this:

```
1. If Request.Form("email") <> "" Then
2. If Request.Form("email").Count = 0 Then
```

In method 1 the check simply tests if the value of the string is not equal to (<>) nothing (quotation marks with no content between them). Method 2 is a little more refined, using the count property. If the count is zero, then the string is empty.

CHANGING VARIABLE TYPES

When a variable is assigned a value, it is often also assigned a type (or subtype). However, sometimes the type is not what we would like, in which case a little force must be used to re-assign the type. Although numbers sit comfortably in variables of type string (provided the text does not begin with a number), it is clearly not very intelligent to try to assign type = integer to a variable that contains the word "text." In practice, a major problem occurs when pure numerical values are in variables that have acquired the type string and that must be reassigned to type = integer (or single or double or byte) in order to use it in an operation.

The following example reviews the most common conversion functions. In actuality, both VBScript and JScript provide many such functions.

Example L: Changing Variables from Text to Numbers and back Again

1. Open your HTML editor and type the following:

```
<HTML>
<HEAD></HEAD>
<BODY>
<%
pi = "3,142"
stringvalue=TypeName(pi)
Response.Write pi & " is a variable type " & stringvalue & "<BR>"
doubvalue = CDbl(pi)
Response.Write doubvalue & "  That was double from string<BR>"
integervalue1 = CInt(doubvalue)
Response.Write integervalue1 & "  That was integer from double<BR>"
integervalue2= CInt(pi)
Response.Write integervalue2 & "  That was integer from string<BR>"
retvalue = CStr(integervalue2)
Response.Write retvalue & "  And that was string again from integer<BR>"
stringvalue2=TypeName(retvalue)
Response.Write stringvalue2 & _
" (Just checking that the last variable really was a string!)"
%>
</BODY>
</HTML>
```

2. Save the document as C:\inetpub\wwwroot\converting.asp.

3. Open your browser and type **http://localhost/converting.asp** in the address line.

Explanation

In pi = "3,142" the quotation marks define pi to be a string variable. Note that if you write the decimal number with a point, the point will be thrown out of the string and it will be accepted as 3142.

We can write pi as a double by leaving out the quotation marks. But in that case, we would need to write it with a decimal point and not a comma (pi = 3.142). To make the situation more complicated, when it is written with a point, the browser shows the decimal point as a comma!

TypeName(pi) is used to find out the variable's type. Notice the use of TypeName here to achieve the same result as the use of varType in Example E. The conversion is achieved using C (for "convert") and shorthand for the type you want to convert to:

```
doubvalue = CDbl(pi)
```

with the name of the variable in question in parentheses. Here we use CDbl, CInt, and CStr. A table of further useful conversions is given below.

Be careful when converting. Notice that the double value of pi is 3.142, and upon conversion to integer all information after the decimal point is lost (i.e., pi is 3). This information cannot be retrieved again when the integer is converted back to string (or to double).

Table 6: Conversions

Function	Description
CBool	Returns the Boolean (True/False) value
CByte	Converts to byte (for whole numbers up to 255)
CCur	Converts to currency
CDate	Converts to date
CDbl	Converts to decimal
CSng	Converts to single
CInt	Converts to integer
CLng	Converts to long
DateSerial	Converts numerical date to text
TimeSerial	Returns the hour, minute, and second
Hex	Returns a string containing the hexadecimal of a number
Sgn	Returns the sign (positive or negative) of a number
CStr	Converts to string

CONVERSION WITH JAVASCRIPT

Example M: Calling a JavaScript Function from VBScript and Using It for Server-side Variable Conversion

1. Open your HTML editor and type the following:

```
<%@ Language=VBScript %>

<script language="JavaScript" runat="server">
function pInt(pvalue,pindex)
{
return parseInt(pvalue,pindex)
}
</script>
<HTML>
<HEAD></HEAD>
<BODY>

<%
Response.Write pInt("1a") & "<BR>"
Response.Write pInt("1a",16) & "<BR>"
Response.Write pInt("101a",2) & "<BR>"
%>

</BODY>
</HTML>
```

2. Save the document as C:\inetpub\wwwroot\function.asp.

3. Start your browser and type **http://localhost/function.asp** in the address field.

Explanation

If you check and find that the client is using a version 4.75 browser, you may wish to shorten this to 4 (because if you want to redirect them to a version-optimized script, then you only care whether they have version 3, 4, or 5 browsers). To do this you can use the JavaScript method parseInt( ).

```
<script language="JavaScript" runat="server">
function pInt(pvalue,pindex)
{
return parseInt(pvalue,pindex);
}
</script>
```

This defines the function. This function is called simultaneously while Response.Write pInt("1a") & "<BR>" writes to the browser. 1a returns the whole number in decimal system (i.e., base 10, the default standard) number 1. (Notice that it removes the "a.") pInt("1a",16) returns the whole number in base 16 (hexadecimal), and pInt("101",2) returns the whole number in binary (base 2). Unfortunately, JavaScript is not good at conversions. However, strings can be converted to decimal numbers using the function parseFloat() and numbers to strings using the function toString().

SENDING VARIABLES BETWEEN FILES

Variables are sent in name/value pairs; that is, the variable's name and the value it contains are sent together. The two methods of sending are using a URL (to the second file) and using a form (where the ACTION points to the second file). The name/value pairs are recovered again using Request.QueryString or Request.Form, respectively.

Example N: Creating Two Files—The Data Is Typed in the First (.htm) File Then Sent via a FORM to the Second (.asp) File

1. Open your HTML editor and type the following:

```
<%@ Language=VBScript%>
<HTML>
<HEAD><TITLE>Order Form</TITLE></HEAD>
<BODY>
<H1>Order some socks ...</H1>
<P>Please fill out the following order form and click
on "send"</P>
<FORM ACTION="form.asp" METHOD="POST">
<B>Gender:</B>
<INPUT TYPE="radio" value="Male" name="gender">Man
<INPUT TYPE="radio" value="Female" name="gender">Woman<P>
<B>Size:</B>
<INPUT TYPE="TEXT" WIDTH="20" NAME="size" size="4"><P>
<B>Color:</B>
<SELECT size="1" name="color">
<OPTION>Blue</OPTION>
<OPTION>Green</OPTION>
<OPTION>Black</OPTION>
</SELECT><P>
<INPUT TYPE="SUBMIT" VALUE="Send Order">
</FORM>
</BODY>
</HTML>
```

2. Save the document as C:\inetpub\wwwroot\form.htm.

3. Open your HTML editor again and type the following:

```
<%@ Language=VBScript%>
<HTML>
<BODY>
<H1>Confirmation of Order ...</H1>
<B>You ordered the following:</B><P>
<%
Dim strgen, strsize, strcol
strgen = Request.Form("gender")
intsize = Request.Form("size")
strcol = Request.Form("color")
Response.Write "Your gender: " & strgen & "<BR>"
Response.Write "Your size: " & intsize & "<BR>"
Response.Write "The color you ordered: " & strcol & "<BR>"
%>
</BODY>
</HTML>
```

4. Save the document as C:\inetpub\wwwroot\form.asp.

5. Start your browser and type **http://localhost/form.htm** in the address field.

6. Fill out the order form and click the **Submit** button.

Explanation

```
<FORM ACTION="form.asp" METHOD="POST">
```
Form.asp is the file that handles the data. The method is set to POST and the name/value pairs are generated in the input fields, for example:

```
<INPUT TYPE="radio" value="Male" name="gender">
```

The data is received in the file form.asp with, for example, strgen = Request.Form("gender"). Notice the name of the new variable, which assumes the value of the variable gender. It is useful to call it strgen, so we can better recall that it is string gender. The integer content of the variable size is assigned to the new variable named intsize—again, purely so we can remember it better.

THE FORM METHODS POST AND GET

The GET method sends the data via URL to HEAD of the receiving file. The name/value pairs are simply tagged onto the back of the URL, separated by a ? sign. For example:

```
http://localhost/form.asp?gender=male&size=45&color=blue
```

This is a relatively fast method, but HEAD can only hold 1,024 bytes. And most older browsers can't deal with URLs more than 255 characters in length. Another problem is that the data being sent is quite openly displayed. This could become a safety issue, although it may be convenient for going back and recovering individual pages. For example, this could be useful for retrieving previous results from search engines.

For these reasons the method POST is normally preferred when sending forms. POST sends information as unencrypted simple text too, but the results are not openly displayed, are independent of the URL length, and are written to BODY.

Home Exercise 1 (this should take you a whole day)

Make a simple system for ordering boards from a lumber shop. Customers can order boards in round feet (1, 2, 3, etc., not anything like 5.44), choose from at least three types of wood (each type has a different price), and choose between picking it up themselves or having it delivered. If they want it delivered, the price is $2 per mile (distances in miles are rounded down). Finally, when the customer clicks on "order," then the information is reviewed and the price with and without tax is displayed.

ARRAYS

Arrays are data holders, much like tables.

Example O: A Simple Array

1. Open your HTML editor and type the following:

```
<%@ Language=VBScript%>
<HTML>
<HEAD><TITLE>Array</TITLE></HEAD>
<BODY BGCOLOR="lightblue">
<H1>24 Hour Grill Bar</H1>
<%
Dim menu(5,1)

Response.Write "The time is now: " & _
Hour(Now) & ":" & Minute(Now) & "<P>"

menu(0,0)="Burger"
menu(1,0)="Hot Dog"
menu(2,0)="Sandwich"
menu(3,0)="Pizza 1"
menu(4,0)="Pizza 2"
menu(5,0)="Pizza 3"

menu(0,1)=6
menu(1,1)=2
menu(2,1)=3
menu(3,1)=4
menu(4,1)=5
menu(5,1)=6

For i=0 to Ubound(menu)
Response.Write "<B>" & menu(i,0) & _
"</B> Price: " & menu (i,1) & "$<BR>"
Next
%>

</BODY>
</HTML>
```

2. Save the document as
    C:\inetpub\wwwroot\array.asp.

3. Start your browser and type **http://localhost/
    array.asp** in the address field.

Explanation

The syntax for making the table

Burger	6
Hot Dog	2
Sandwich	3
Pizza 1	4
Pizza 2	5
Pizza 3	6

is Dim menu(5,1).

The first number in parentheses indicates the first dimension (row number), and the second number indicates the second dimension (column number). Numbering begins with 0 (zero). Therefore the most simple table that can be made is Dim menu(1,1). To put a string value in the first row, first column, write menu(0,0) = "Burger". To put an integer value in the same row of the second column, write menu(0,1) = 6. Arrays can be resized both larger and smaller. If we want to resize a table so it is larger, we can use ReDim menu(10,1), but in this case the original values are lost. If you want to preserve the original values in a larger table you must use ReDim Preserve(10,1). All resizing to a smaller table results in loss of all of the original values, whether you use Preserve or not!

`Ubound(menu)`

Ubound returns the number of rows in the table (the array variable menu). In this case Ubound will return 5. Thus the statement `For i=0 to Ubound` means that the data is examined 6 times, with values of i being 0, 1, 2, 3, 4 and 5. These are then put in the Response.Write both as menu(i,0) and as menu(i,1), resulting in each row being written out.

Home Exercise 2
(this should take you a whole day)

Make a Web site for a grill/burger bar offering the options from the above exercise. Between 10 a.m. and 9 p.m. the site should have a yellow background color and a blue text color. Outside this time the site should have a navy background color and a white text color, prices should be 50% higher, and it should not be possible to order a sandwich.

COOKIES

A cookie is a small text file that the browser saves to the client's hard disk (either in C:\windows \temporary internet files or in C:\windows \cookies). Most cookies have a specified lifetime, from 1 minute up to 50 years. In browsers like Internet Explorer and Netscape Navigator the clients themselves can choose if they wish to accept cookies or not. Since ASP functionality (the Session object, which we will return to later) requires cookies, it can be a good idea if the client, upon entry into an ASP Web site, is confronted with a message explaining that it is necessary to accept cookies.

The core of the programming can be summed up as follows:

- To write input to a cookie—Response.Cookies("name") = "Fred Bloggs"

- To read a cookie—strVariableName = Request.Cookies("name")

Example P: Writing Information to a Cookie

1. Open your HTML editor and type the following:

```
<%@ Language=VBScript%>
<%
firstname = Request.Cookies("info")("firstname")
lastname = Request.Cookies("info")("lastname")
address = Request.Cookies("info")("address")
zipcode = Request.Cookies("info")("zipcode")
town = Request.Cookies("info")("town")
telephone = Request.Cookies("info")("telephone")
email = Request.Cookies("info")("email")
%>

<HTML>
<HEAD>
</HEAD>
<BODY>
<H2>Order Form:</H2>

<FORM METHOD="POST" ACTION="makeCookie.asp">
First Name:<BR>
<INPUT TYPE="text" name="firstname" value="<%=firstname%>"><BR>
Last Name:<BR>
<INPUT TYPE="text" name="lastname" value="<%=lastname%>"><BR>
Address:<BR>
<INPUT TYPE="text" name="address" size="40" value="<%=address%>"><BR>
```

```
Zip Code:<BR>
<INPUT TYPE="text" name="zipcode" size="6" value="<%=zipcode%>"><BR>
Town:<BR>
<INPUT TYPE="text" name="town" value="<%=town%>"><BR>
Telephone:<BR>
<INPUT TYPE="text" name="telephone" size="10" value="<%=telephone%>">
<BR>
Email:<BR>
<INPUT TYPE="text" name="email" value="<%=email%>"><BR>
<INPUT TYPE="submit" name="Send" value="Send">
</FORM>
</BODY>
</HTML>
```

2. Save the document as C:\inetpub\wwwroot\formCookies.asp.

3. Open your HTML editor and type the following:

```
<%@ Language=VBScript%>
<%
Response.Cookies("info")("firstname") = Request.Form("firstname")
Response.Cookies("info")("lastname") = Request.Form("lastname")
Response.Cookies("info")("address") = Request.Form("address")
Response.Cookies("info")("zipcode") = Request.Form("zipcode")
Response.Cookies("info")("town") = Request.Form("town")
Response.Cookies("info")("telephone") = Request.Form("telephone")
Response.Cookies("info")("email") = Request.Form("email")

'now we write that information to the cookie
'specifying its lifetime

Response.Cookies("info").Expires = Date + 90
```

```
%>

<HTML>
<BODY>
Thank you for your order ...<P>
The Cookie has been set ...<P>
</BODY>
</HTML>
```

4. Save the document as C:\inetpub\wwwroot\makeCookie.asp.

5. Start your browser and type **http://localhost/formCookies.asp** in the address field.

6. Fill out the form and click on **Send**.

7. Find the file yourPCname.txt or localhost.txt (it will probably be in C:\windows\temporary internet files, with a copy in C:\windows\cookies) and open it in Notepad or other ASCII text editor.

   Cookies look like this:

   ```
   TELEPHONE=45+39613585&TOWN=Hellerup&ZIPCODE=DK%2D2900 ...
   ```

   You can see that the information is stored in a string of name/value pairs separated by & signs, exactly as you can see when the data is sent using the URL method.

APPLICATIONS AND SESSIONS

A session starts when a user (client) queries an ASP file in a server application. A session is "owned" by a user (the client's browser). Therefore it is essential that the server knows when a session has begun and when it is ended. This is done by means of sending a cookie to the client, which contains a SessionID. Therefore it is also essential that the client accepts cookies (Internet Explorer 5.5 makes it harder for clients to refuse cookies—this option is no longer given explicitly under the Advanced options but rather is buried under the browser's Safety options). As an ASP programmer, it is useful to know if a client accepts cookies or not. The most used method is simply to check if the client has any cookies and assume that if they already have some, then they accept cookies. The following script checks for cookies and, if none are found, uses Response.Redirect to redirect the client to a special document.

```
StartSide= "default.htm"
'the default.htm contains an explanation
'of the consequences of refusing cookies
If Len(CStr(Request.ServerVariables("HTTP_COOKIES")))=0 Then
HereSide = Request.ServerVariables("SCRIPT_NAME")
If Not strComp(HereSide, StartSide, 0) Then
Response.Redirect(StartSide)
End If
```

All objects activated or created by a session can be reset to zero (that is, finished) either using Timeout (session.TimeOut, the default value is 20) or directly and immediately using Session.Abandon.

An application is associated with the physical structure of application starting points (as defined by IIS). An application is defined as all ASP files in a virtual directory (including subdirectories) providing that that virtual directory has been defined as an application starting point. Thus applications are bound to the server, and not to the client (as we saw is the case for sessions). Therefore, it is rare to actively use application objects. If they are used, they are written into the file global.asa.

Global.asa (the "asa" stands for "active server applications") is an optional file that always lies in the Web root. It can contain definitions of global objects, functions, and procedures. Such defined components can be used in the whole of the application scope and be freely called from all ASP files in that application.

One possible use of an application object in a function within global.asa could be, for example, counting visits. The following script would activate upon each client visit (session_OnStart).

```
<script runat="server" Language="VBScript">
Sub Application_OnStart
Application.Contents("visit")=0
End sub
Sub session_OnStart
Application.Contents("visit")= visit + 1
End sub
Sub session_OnEnd
Application.Contents("visit")= visit - 1
End sub
</script>
```

PASSWORD-PROTECTED LOGS

Password protection is very useful. However, real protection is fairly complicated, involving a database on a secure server. There are also many "mini-solutions" available in JavaScript and other languages where an input is simply compared to a list contained in another Internet document. These are relatively unsafe because JavaScript can be read in the browser source. A reasonable improvement (but still not perfect) can be achieved using ASP, because the ASP code is not displayed in the browser source. The following example concerns the use of the session object, introduces two properties of the Response object (Buffer and Redirect), and introduces included files.

Example Q: Logging On Using Session Variables and an Included (.inc) File

This example uses five files. The first input file is logon.htm. The input data is sent to menu.asp where it is compared with a given password. If the password corresponds with the input, then the session variable is accepted (either for 20 minutes or so long as the file is active in the browser window) and menu.asp is shown. If it does not correspond, the user is sent back to logon.htm. In menu.asp a link is shown to check.asp. In check.asp, not the password, but the session status, is checked. Using two further files we then try to call a file to check again if the user is logged on. This file uses a script embedded in an included file, logon.inc.

1. Open your HTML editor and type the following:

```
<HTML>
<HEAD>
</HEAD>
<BODY>
<H1>Log On:</H1>
<FORM METHOD="POST" ACTION="menu.asp">
<INPUT TYPE="password" name="password" size="20"><P>
<INPUT TYPE="submit" value="Log On"><P>
</FORM>
</BODY>
</HTML>
```

2. Save the document as C:\inetpub\wwwroot\logon.htm.

3. Type in a new file in the HTML editor:

```
<%@ Language=VBScript%>
<%
Response.Buffer = true
%>
```

```
<HTML>
<HEAD>
</HEAD>

<BODY>
<%
pass = Lcase(Request.Form("password"))
If pass <> "therightpassword" Then
Response.Clear
Response.Redirect "logon.htm"
Else
Session("ok") = true
End If
%>
<H1>Welcome to Menu.ASP</H1>

<A HREF="check1.asp">Check1.asp: Check your session status
here</A><BR>
<A HREF="check2.asp">Check2.asp: Check your session status
here using included file</A>

</BODY>
</HTML>
```

4. Save the document as C:\inetpub\wwwroot\menu.asp.

Explanation for the First Part

First in menu.asp we write Response.Buffer = true. By default, buffer is turned off, so it has to be expressly set to "true" to use it. Buffer is a temporary memory space used to store the results of the script. If the results of the script are correct, then the results of the check (i.e., all code up to the last %> sign) are printed. If the password is wrong, then the contents of the buffer are erased using Response.Clear before any HTML is shown to the client. The Buffer property has three methods—Clear, Flush, and End. Calling these results in a run-time error if Buffer has not been set to true. The Flush method (Response.Flush) can be very useful in sending previously buffered output to the client while still processing the script, for example, sending partial results of a long search.

For ease of handling the password, input is converted to lowercase letters using

```
Lcase(Request.Form("password"))
```

Note that the syntax for saving a session variable can be

- Session("ok") = true,

- Session("name") = "Fred Bloggs", or even

- Session("username") = Request.Form("username").

5. In a new file in the HTML editor, type the following:

```
<%@ Language=VBScript%>
<%
If session("ok") = false Then
Response.Redirect "logon.htm"
End If
%>
<HTML>
```

```
<BODY>
<H1>You are logged on</H1>
</BODY>
</HTML>
```

6. Save the document as C:\inetpub\wwwroot\check1.asp.

7. Open http://localhost/logon.htm in your browser. Try to log on with the wrong password, then with the correct password, therightpassword (you can mix capital and small letters). Once you can see menu.asp, click on **check1.asp**.

Explanation for the Second Part

The Response.Redirect used here contains a relative path. Absolute paths can also be used, e.g., Response.Redirect "http://anywebsite.com/anyfile.htm". Similar methods include Server.Execute and Server.Transfer. Server.Execute(pagename) transfers execution over to that file, executes, then returns to the original page. Server.Transfer (pagename) is similar, except that it stays at the second page.

In check1.asp the IF statement checks whether the Session("ok") variable is set to true or not. If the variable is "false," then the user is sent back to the first side to input again.

It is important to note that this is not a password check, but purely a session variable check. This means that all files "behind" the password check can be protected, even if a returning client jumps directly to their specific URLs.

To build on this, the next part of the example shows that you don't even need to write the code in its entirety to all the "behind" files you're protecting. ASP allows for included source files, just as in Java (.class source files), in Cascading Style Sheets (.css source files), and in JavaScript (.js source files). In ASP these are called .inc files.

8. In a new file in the HTML editor type the following:

```
<!-- #include file="logon.inc" -->
<HTML>
<BODY>
Check 2: You are logged on
</BODY>
</HTML>
```

9. Save the document as C:\inetpub\wwwroot\check2.asp.

10. In a new file in the HTML editor type the following:

```
<%@ Language=VBScript%>
<%
```

```
If Session("ok") = false Then
Response.Redirect "logon.htm"
End If
%>
```

11. Save the document as C:\inetpub\wwwroot\logon.inc.

12. Return to logon.htm and log on. At menu.asp click on **check2.asp**. Now boot your PC. When it is running again, open the browser and type **http://localhost/check2.asp** in the address field.

Explanation for the Third Part

Once you have booted your PC (shutting Personal Web Server down), then the session object has expired. You have just seen the content of check2.asp (after logging on), but now the session object is false. You cannot come in again (nor to check1.asp), but you keep being sent back to logon.htm for your password.

The difference between check1.asp and check2.asp is that the code that does the checking is external in check2.asp. Thus, one can have the check in an external file (.inc source file) and simply refer to it from all the files that you wish to protect. This means you only need to type one short line of code in each of the protected files.

The syntax to call .inc source files is

```
#include file="filename.inc"
```

When ASP sees #include (in small or capital letters), it looks for the file argument, which specifies the SSI (Server Side Include) or which file is to be included. The contents of the SSI behave exactly as if they were typed directly into the first file. The .inc file may contain many things, for example the session variable check (like above), subroutines (see later examples), or flat HTML, if you want to repeat, for example, headers or footers on all your pages.

DEBUGGING

It is doubtful that anyone has ever written an ASP Web site that worked perfectly the first time. Therefore it's a good idea to review how to debug. In this section we will look at some methods commonly used to find errors. These include

- Option Explicit

- Structured code and comments

- Variable names

- Response.Write

- On Error Resume Next

Option Explicit

Writing <% Option Explicit %> at the beginning of an ASP document means that all variables must be declared before use.

Example:

```
<% Option Explicit %>
<%
Dim firstname, lastname
name = "Fred"
%>
```

This code will result in VBScript error 800a01f4, informing you that

```
Variable not defined: 'name'
filename.asp, line 4
```

Notice that line numbers (as in JavaScript and other languages, but not in HTML) include empty lines. In the third line the variables firstname and lastname are declared using dimension (Dim). However, the variable name on line four has not been declared. Option Explicit helps to find typos, simple spelling mistakes. It is easy to Dim firstname, and later accidentally try to call firstnme or frstname.

Structured Code and Comments

You should set up code so it is easy to read six months later (or so your associates can read it easily). At regular intervals (or to explain any unusual code) put in comments to explain what is happening and why.

Example:

```
If Request.Form("A") > 17 and Request.Form("A") < 68 Then Response.Write "Welcome" End If
```

would be better written

```
If Request.Form("A") > 17
And Request.Form("A") < 68 Then
Response.Write "Welcome"
End If
```

Variable Names

Make your variable names mean something. Instead of

```
Dim A
A = Request.Form("field")
If inStr(A, "@") and inStr(A(, ".") > 0 Then
Response.Write "Ok"
Else
Response.Write "Not"
End If
```

try

```
Dim strAddress
strAddress = Request.Form("frmEmail")
If inStr(strAddress, "@") and inStr(strAddress, ".") > 0 Then
Response.Write "Ok"
Else
Response.Write "Not"
End If
```

Here the variable name is understandable and implies which type of variable it is (or should be). If the problem persists, make sure that your variable name is not a reserved word.

Response.Write (and Debug.inc)

The classical method of debugging is to Response.Write often. Messages can be displayed at various points during the code, simply to see how far you have gotten. Similarly you can check the value of variables at various points.

Example:

```
intNr = Request.Form("frmShoeNr")
Response.Write intNr
If intNr = 43 Then ...
```

This is useful because the error may actually be on the preceding page. Think if, in the above example, the input field should have been frmShoeSize, but we took frmShoeNr by mistake. By extension we can put a Response.Write-based code in an included file and simply refer to it at various points in the code. For example,

```
Function Debug(var)
Select Case varType(var)
Case 0
Response.Write "<B>Debug:</B> " & var & "<BR>"
Response.Write "<LI>Variable not defined<P>"
Case 8
Response.Write "<B>Debug:</B> " & var & "<BR>"
Response.Write "<LI>String variable<P>"
Case Else
Response.Write "<B>Unknown type</B><LI>" & var
End Select
End Function
```

Save the above code to debug.inc and then call the debug function at the relevant points in your code by writing

```
<!-- #include file="debug.inc" -->
```

On Error Resume Next

Just after <%, at the top of the code, write

```
On Error Resume Next
```

followed by the code that needs debugging. Errors are "ignored" inasmuch as the server now tries to execute the remaining scripts (if possible). At the end of the code block write

```
GetLastError()
```

This returns a reference to an ASPError object with details of the last error occurring in asp.dll. The information includes file name, line number, and error code.

ASP AND DATABASES

One of the enormous advantages ASP has over flat HTML is its ability to retrieve data from databases and show it in a browser.

One example of this could be prices on a Web site. Perhaps the price of a certain product is shown in six different places. However, each data field contains no HTML, but simply refers to a database record. Thus, when the record is updated, all six HTML files show the new price.

ASP can connect with databases using various methods. They vary with respect to Data Source Name (DSN).

Table 7: Methods to connect with databases

A DSN Connection to Access	A DSN-less Connection to Access	A DSN-less Connection to SQL
"dsn=dsnODBC"	strConnect = "Driver={Microsoft Access Driver (*.MDB)}; DBQ=" & Server.MapPath ("northwind.mdb")	StrConnect="Driver={SQL Server}; Server=servername;UID=user ID; PWD=password"
This type of connection can only be used in your PC or in a LAN where the driver is installed on each PC.	Notice that the database query (DBQ) uses a MapPath. This is the relative path from the ASP file to the database file. For example, MapPath("/dir/northwind.mdb") means C:\inetpub\wwwroot\ dir\northwind.mdb.	Here the driver and SQL server are specified, together with the ID and password needed to log on.
Access is not normally used on the Internet, both because the files are relatively large and also because Access becomes slow when many users are in simultaneously. However, Access can sometimes be an excellent solution, for example, with a medium-size firm's intranet.		SQL server 7 on an NT4 platform together with an Internet Information Server (IIS) would be a standard software mix for commercial Internet uses.

All of the following examples use an Access database. This is northwind.mdb, a standard example database included in the Access part of the MS Office package. Find northwind.mdb and copy it to C:\inetpub\wwwroot. Normally this file is not write-protected. If it is, either remove the protection or, if you are using it on the Web, write the above string (DSN-less!) plus `password=' '`, including the real password in the single quotes.

The first of the following examples uses a DSN connection. Subsequent examples use DSN-less connections. A DSN connection has to be made in Open Database Connectivity (ODBC). ODBC is a kind of standard language that can communicate with all types of databases. In the case of our first example, an ODBC driver has to be installed. Just as in installing a printer driver, where the driver is installed after pointing the program at a specific printer, ODBC has to be pointed at a specific database. This means that if you use several databases, you have to install the ODBC driver several times, where each connection has a unique name.

Open northwind.mdb in Access and check that all fields accept zero length. Close Access and check that the database file is writable. (In the PC, right-click and look under **Properties**. On NT4 check that the user group "everyone" has write rights. This is equivalent to CHMOD 777 on Unix.)

SETTING UP AN ODBC CONNECTION

To work with a DSN Recordset, an ODBC connection has to be established with the server; in this case with your own PC, because you are working with Personal Web Server. Once the connection is established you can concentrate on working in SQL. SQL stands for Structured Query Language and is a command language used to communicate with databases. The SQL lines in ASP are translated by ODBC to a language Access can understand. Using the appropriate ODBC driver you can communicate with Access and all other types of databases. In Control Panel, double-click on the icon **ODBC** and then on **System DSN**.

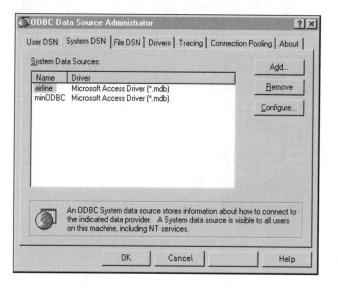

Here you see that drivers to two databases are already installed. The connections (not the databases) are called "airline" and "minODBC." If we were to click on **Configure**, we would see that neither of these connections point to northwind.mdb. Therefore a new connection is needed; click on **Add**. This creates a new database source, as shown below.

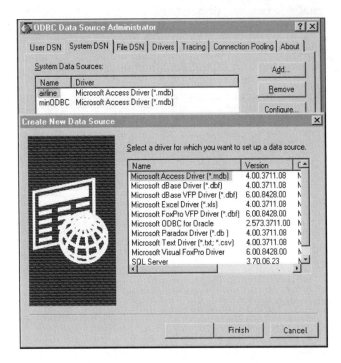

As you can see, drivers connecting to many different types of databases are available. You should select the first item, **Microsoft Access Driver**.

The next menu asks you to select the correct database. In this case, browse to the correct one. Here you can see that northwind.mdb actually is in a subdirectory (engasp) of the PWS. Select the correct database (in this case **northwind.mdb**) and click on **OK**. There can be only one database per connection.

The ODBC setup then returns an information menu. The path to the database is recorded. (If you have made a mistake and wish to change it, click

Select and repeat the process.) In the field above, type in a Data Source Name. This can be almost any name, providing it is unique, meaning that no two connections can have the same name.

It is a good idea to call connections "somethingODBC," as this makes them easier to find in the ASP code. In this case the new connection to northwind.mdb is called "demoODBC."

Click **OK** and the connection is added to the list of established connections. You can see below that demoODBC is now in the list, alongside the original two connections, airline and minODBC.

Click **OK** and the DSN connection is ready for use.

DATABASE MANIPULATION

Example R1: Using DSN to Show the Content of a Database in HTML

1. Open the HTML editor and type the following:

```
<%@ Language=VBScript%>
<HTML>
<HEAD>
</HEAD>
<BODY>
<H1>All Product Categories</H1>
<%
Dim objRec
Set objRec = Server.CreateObject ("ADODB.Recordset")
objRec.Open "SELECT * FROM Categories", "dsn=demoODBC"
Do While Not objRec.EOF
Response.Write "<B>" & objRec("Category Name") & "<BR></B>"
Response.Write "Category ID:<B> " & objRec("Category ID") & "<BR>"
Response.Write "</B>Description: <B>" & objRec("Description") & "</B>"
objRec.MoveNext
Response.Write "<HR WIDTH='300' HEIGHT='1'>"
Loop
objRec.Close
Set objRec = Nothing
%>
</BODY>
</HTML>
```

2. Save the document as C:\inetpub\wwwroot\showall.asp.

3. Start your browser and type **http://localhost/showall.asp** in the address field.

If you have problems, open the database in Access, highlight each column, right-click, choose **Rename**, and check that there are no spaces in the column name. Try again.

If the column you are interested in has a space in its name, then in the SQL command string (but not in Response.Write), the name has to be in single quotation marks, e.g., `'Category ID'`.

Explanation

```
Recordset
Set objRec = Server.CreateObject ("ADODB.Recordset")
```
Here a new instance of the object ADO (ActiveX Data Objects) is made. This component helps when making advanced database operations. These objects are always defined with Set.

A Recordset is an object used to work with data from a data source. A Recordset can be compared with a table's rows and columns, where data can be stored and manipulated.

```
objRec.Open "SELECT * FROM categories", "dsn=demoODBC"
```
With the object property Open, the connection to the database named in DSN is opened. Remember there should be no spaces around the equals sign here. This connection remains open until we close it.

"SELECT * FROM categories" contains the SQL command string used in ASP. It is slightly different from that used in Access, meaning that SQL command strings you may take from using Access may have to be modified.

By convention, SQL commands are written in all capital letters, although the lack of case sensitivity means that it is also possible to write commands in lowercase letters. SQL command strings tell the database how to react.

SELECT tells the database file to read data from the database. The method of specifying which data can vary. Basically, to select some columns (of many) from a certain table (remember databases can contain many tables), the following general syntax can be used:

```
SELECT column1, column2 FROM tablename
```

This is a standard method. However, one can also use "dot syntax":

```
SELECT column1.tablename, column2.tablename
```

where the column and table names are joined using a dot. In the above example the wildcard sign (*) is used. It means "all," and is recommended for use in ASP.

The Recordset now contains all the rows and columns from the database and the Recordset's cursor stands in the first row of the table structure. If we were to write it out now, only the first row would be read and shown. Therefore a do loop is used to move the cursor down the table, row by row.

```
Do While Not objRec.EOF
```

EOF is a property of the object Recordset. It is an acronym for "end of file." EOF (as well as BOF—beginning of file) returns Boolean values, true or false. Thus the do loop reiterates as long as EOF is false (the cursor has not reached end of file) and stops when EOF is true.

Using the syntax objRec("columnname"), the value in the field where the cursor stands is picked out and written `Response.Write objRec("columnname")`. This can be concatenated with HTML commands to give a better layout. Notice that as long as the Recordset is open, data can be extracted in any sequence or left alone, unused. In the example the order is Category Name, Category ID, and Description, but in the database file the column order is Category ID, Category Name, Description, and Picture. This is a useful method; SELECT all the data but "filter out" the columns you don't need in the ASP file.

Using objRec.MoveNext the cursor is simply moved one row down in the Recordset. It is important to remember this, because otherwise the do loop will never reach EOF, but will continue endlessly.

```
objRec.Close
Set objRec = Nothing
```

In these lines the Recordset that was opened in line 10 is closed, and the connection to the database (the ActiveX Data Object) is eliminated (using Set again to equate it with Nothing). These lines are important, because leaving the database open takes up server memory and occupies the database for other sessions.

Notice that attempting to recover data, for example using objRec("columnname"), after closing the connection, will no longer work.

Example R2: Searching a Database without DSN—Using a DSN-less Connection

1. Open your HTML editor and type the following:

```
<%@ Language=VBScript%>
<% t = Request.Form("n") %>
<HTML>
<HEAD></HEAD>
<BODY>
<% If t = "" Then %>
<H1>Search for Suppliers by Country or Telephone Number:</H1>
<FORM ACTION="search.asp" METHOD="post">
<INPUT TYPE="TEXT" NAME="n"><BR>
Criteria are <B>Country</B> or <B>Phone Number</B><P>
<INPUT TYPE="SUBMIT" VALUE="Search">
</FORM><BR><BR>
<% Else %>
```

```
<H1>Information:</H1>
<%
Dim objRec
strConnect = "Driver={Microsoft Access Driver (*.MDB)}; _
DBQ="& Server.MapPath("northwind.mdb")
Set objRec = Server.CreateObject("ADODB.Recordset")
objRec.Open "SELECT * FROM Suppliers WHERE Country = '" & _
t & "' OR Phone = '" & t & "'", strConnect
Do While Not objRec.EOF
countup = countup + 1
objRec.MoveNext
Loop
If countup > 0 Then
Response.Write "<B>There have been " & countup & " hits</B><P>"
objRec.MoveFirst
Do While Not objRec.EOF
Response.Write "<B>" & objRec("Company Name") & " " & _
objRec("Contact Name") Response.Write "</B><BR>Address: <B>" & _
objRec("Address")
Response.Write "</B><BR>City: <B>" & objRec("City")
Response.Write "</B><BR>Zip Code: <B>" & objRec("Postal Code")
Response.Write "</B><BR>Country: <B>" & objRec("Country")
Response.Write "</B><BR>Phone: <B>" & objRec("Phone")
Response.Write "</B><BR>Fax: <B>" & objRec("Fax")
Response.Write "</B><HR HEIGHT='1' WIDTH='250' ALIGN='left'>"
objRec.MoveNext
Loop
Else
Response.Write "Sorry, no one found!<P>"
End If
objRec.Close
```

```
Set objRec = Nothing %>
<% End If %>
</BODY>
</HTML>
```

2. Save the document as
   C:\inetpub\wwwroot\search.asp.

3. Start your browser and type **http://localhost/
   search.asp** in the address field.

Explanation

The first line of the ASP script has two functions. It ensures that if the variable t is empty (which it is upon the client's first visit), then the client is shown the input form.

```
<% If  t = "" Then %>
```

If the variable t is not empty, then the input form is not shown, but rather the database is searched for matches to the content of t, and the results printed to the screen. This is the part that comes after

```
<% Else %>
```

The Recordset variable is first declared, then the DSN-less path to the database. After that the ADOBD object is created. Using this database connection, the SQL command string can be executed. The SQL syntax now introduces OR (and AND).

```
SELECT columnnames FROM tablename WHERE
criterion1 OR/AND criterion2
```

Criterion1 is the text string content of the variable t. If you specified columnname as "Country" and t was "Germany," data would be returned only where the data field in the column "Country" exactly matched "Germany." The next section explains how to widen your search.

A counter is built in, using a do while loop:

```
Do While Not objRec.EOF
countup = countup + 1
objRec.MoveNext
Loop
```

This simply adds 1 to the numerical value of the variable countup each time the cursor moves down a row in the Recordset, until EOF is reached. Thus the value of countup is the number of hits. This is a very useful method, but you must remember that the cursor is on the end row of the database table. Thus the second search will be empty because objRec.EOF is true. In order to search again the cursor has to be reset to BOF. This is done using MoveFirst.

As in Example Q, the connection is closed and the Recordset object eliminated using

```
objRec.Close
Set objRec = Nothing
%>
```

Widening Your Search with the SQL Wildcard Sign %

In Example R, to find Germany, you would have had to type exactly Germany. Because this exact syntax is clumsy and not very useful, an SQL wildcard percent sign (%) is often used:

```
objRec.Open "SELECT * FROM Suppliers WHERE Country LIKE '%" & _
t & "%'", strConnect
```

The % signs on each side of the variable denote that the rest of the text string can be anything. For example, if you had previously typed in UK, you would have gotten only UK, and U would have given no results. Now, however, simply typing U alone will return everything with a U in it, e.g., UK and USA, as well as Australia (notice the U in Australia).

Instead of using the % sign in the SQL command string, it can be added to the variable:

```
<% t = Request.Form("n")
y = "%" & t & "%"
%>
```

The string looks like

```
SELECT * FROM Suppliers WHERE Country LIKE '" & y & "'
```

However, this method is not recommended, as it is easy to make mistakes (e.g., y = "% & t & %" will always return "no one found," as y now contains the text % & t & %). Furthermore it is hard for the programmer to remember which variables have been "generalized" in this way.

Notice also that to use this syntax, the equals sign (=, meaning exactly identical with) has to be replaced with the less stringent command LIKE.

Example S: Inserting Data into a Database Using Request.Form and INSERT

In this example the input is in an HTML file called add.htm. The form calls addnow.asp, which contains the codes needed to insert a new row into the table "Employees."

1. Open your HTML editor and type the following:

```
<HTML>
<HEAD></HEAD>
<BODY>
<H1>Setting up a new employee in the table "Employees"</H1>
This is a pure HTML input form <BR>.
<TABLE><FORM ACTION="addnow.asp" METHOD="post">
<TR>
<TD><P align=right>Last Name</P></TD>
<TD><INPUT NAME="LastName"></TD>
</TR><TR>
<TD><P align=right>First Name</TD>
<TD><INPUT NAME="FirstName"></TD>
</TR><TR>
<TD><P align=right>Title</P></TD>
<TD><INPUT NAME="Title"></TD>
</TR><TR>
<TD><P align=right>Title Of Courtesy</P></TD>
<TD><INPUT NAME="TitleOfCourtesy"></TD>
</TR><TR>
<TD><P align=right>Date of Birth (date/month/year)</P></TD>
<TD><INPUT NAME="BirthDate"></TD>
</TR><TR>
<TD><P align=right>Starts Work (date/month/year)</P></TD>
<TD><INPUT NAME="HireDate"></TD>
</TR><TR>
```

```
<TD><P align=right>Address</P></TD>
<TD><INPUT NAME="Address"></TD>
</TR><TR>
<TD><P align=right>City</P></TD>
<TD><INPUT NAME="City"></TD>
</TR><TR>
<TD><P align=right>Region</P></TD>
<TD><INPUT NAME="Region"></TD>
</TR><TR>
<TD><P align=right>Zip Code</P></TD>
<TD><INPUT NAME="PostalCode"></TD>
</TR><TR>
<TD><P align=right>Country</P></TD>
<TD><INPUT NAME="Country"></TD>
</TR><TR>
<TD><P align=right>Home Phone</P></TD>
<TD><INPUT NAME="HomePhone"></TD>
</TR><TR>
<TD><P align=right>Extension</P></TD>
<TD><INPUT NAME="Extension"></TD>
</TR><TR>
<TD><P align=right>Notes</P></TD>
<TD><Textarea NAME="Notes"> </textarea></TD>
</TR><TR>
<TD><P align=right>Reports to (number)</P></TD>
<TD><INPUT NAME="ReportsTo"></TD>
</TR><TR><TD> </TD>
<TD><INPUT TYPE="submit" VALUE="Submit">
</TR></FORM></TABLE>
</BODY>
</HTML>
```

2. Save the document as C:\inetpub\wwwroot\add.htm.

3. Open your HTML editor and type the following:

```
<%@ Language=VBScript%>
<HTML>
<BODY>
<%
LastName = Request.Form("LastName")
FirstName = Request.Form("FirstName")
Title = Request.Form("Title")
TitleOfCourtesy = Request.Form("TitleOfCourtesy")
Birth = Request.Form("BirthDate")
Hire = Request.Form("HireDate")
Address = Request.Form("Address")
City = Request.Form("City")
Region = Request.Form("Region")
PostalCode = Request.Form("PostalCode")
Country = Request.Form("Country")
HomePhone = Request.Form("HomePhone")
Extension = Request.Form("Extension")
Notes = Request.Form("Notes")
Reports = Request.Form("ReportsTo")
'Birth, Hire, and Reports are now the wrong type
'of variable so they are converted as follows
BirthDate = CDate(Birth)
HireDate = CDate(Hire)
ReportsTo = CInt(Reports)
'now the table and column names are taken and
'set to the contents of the variables
Dim strSql
strSql = "INSERT INTO Employees
```

```
(LastName,FirstName,Title,TitleOfCourtesy,BirthDate,HireDate,
Address,City,Region,PostalCode,Country,HomePhone,Extension,
Notes,ReportsTo)
VALUES ('" & LastName & "','" & FirstName & "','" & Title & _
"','" & TitleOfCourtesy & "','" & BirthDate & "','" & _
HireDate & "','" & Address & "','" & City & "','" & _
Region & "','" & PostalCode & "','" & Country & "','" & _
HomePhone & "','" & Extension & "','" & Notes & "','" & _
ReportsTo & "')"
Dim objCmd
Set objCmd = Server.CreateObject("ADODB.Command")
objCmd.ActiveConnection = "Driver={Microsoft Access Driver _
(*.MDB)}; DBQ=" & Server.MapPath("northwind.mdb")
objCmd.CommandText = strSql
objCmd.Execute
Set objCmd = Nothing
%>
Thank you for your addition
</BODY>
</HTML>
```

4. Save the document as C:\inetpub\wwwroot\addnow.asp.

5. Start your browser and type **http://localhost/add.htm** in the address field.

Explanation
INSERT INTO tablename (column names separated by commas) VALUES (variable values, `'" & Region & "'`, separated by commas). The order of the column names should correspond to the correct variable for that column.

The INSERT INTO command is used to insert new values into an existing database table. You do not need to put data into every column, except where it is defined as being obligatory in the database.

Remember Auto-numbers (primary key values) are generated automatically.

Command

```
Set objCmd = Server.CreateObject("ADODB.Command")
```

Examples R and Q used the Recordset object. However, here we do not wish to read the existing information into tabular form. Therefore, the active command object Command is used. The command object is used for large, active operations, including INSERT, DELETE, UPDATE in tables, and CREATE (where new tables are generated).

```
objCmd.ActiveConnection = "Driver={Microsoft Access Driver _
(*.MDB)}; DBQ=" & Server.MapPath("northwind.mdb")
```

The ActiveConnection property points to the active database connection (ODBC).

```
objCmd.CommandText = strSql
```

The SQL command string is included in the variable strSql. This is given to the Command object using its CommandText property.

```
objCmd.Execute
```

The Command object's Execute property executes the SQL command string contained in CommandText on the database specified in ActiveConnection. After this the Command object is eliminated:

```
Set objCmd = Nothing
```

Example T: Removing Data from a Database Using the URL Method and Request.QueryString

In this example further SQL commands are explored and data is sent by the HREF method as a query string attached to a URL instead of using a form. Thus Request.Form is replaced by Request.QueryString.

1. Open your HTML editor and type the following:

```
<%@ Language=VBScript%>
<HTML>
<BODY>

<% If Request.QueryString("id").Count=0 Then %>
<H1>Click on the Employee you wish to delete</H1>
<%
Dim objRec
Set objRec = Server.CreateObject("ADODB.Recordset")
objRec.Open "SELECT * FROM Employees", "Driver={Microsoft _
Access Driver (*.MDB)}; DBQ=" & Server.MapPath("northwind.mdb")
Do While Not objRec.EOF
Response.Write "<A HREF='delete.asp?id=" & objRec("EmployeeID") & "'>"
Response.Write objRec("FirstName") & " "
Response.Write objRec("LastName") & "</A><BR>"
objRec.MoveNext
Loop
objRec.Close
Set objRec = Nothing

Else
whichone = Request.QueryString("id")
Dim strSql
strSql = "DELETE FROM Employees WHERE EmployeeID = " & whichone
Dim objCmd
```

```
Set objCmd = Server.CreateObject("ADODB.Command")
objCmd.ActiveConnection="Driver={Microsoft Access Driver _
(*.MDB)}; DBQ=" & Server.MapPath("northwind.mdb")
objCmd.CommandText = strSql
Response.Write "Thank you. Employee number " & whichone & " has been deleted"
Response.Write "<BR>Use the browser's Back button and update _
(Refresh) to check this."
objCmd.Execute
Set objCmd = Nothing

End If %>
</BODY>
</HTML>
```

2. Save the document as C:\inetpub\wwwroot\delete.asp.

3. Start your browser and type **http://localhost/delete.asp** in the address field.

Explanation

The idea behind this script is that upon opening the file,

```
<% If Request.QueryString("id").Count=0 Then %>
```

returns true. Therefore, the database table is opened and a list of all data fields in the Recordset (i.e., employees) is shown, with their names as hyperlinks. The hyperlinks can point to any file, but in this case they point back to delete.asp. The most important part is

```
Response.Write "<A HREF='delete.asp?id=" & objRec("EmployeeID") & "'>"
Response.Write objRec("FirstName") & " "
Response.Write objRec("LastName") & "</A><BR>"
```

By clicking on the name, you activate the link back to the same file. However, an ID number has now been added to the URL using

```
?id=" & objRec("EmployeeID")
```
Look at the URL in the address field after you have clicked on a name.

When the file is read in again,

```
<% If Request.QueryString("id").Count=0 Then %>
```
returns false and the ELSE statement is executed instead.

The addition on the end of the URL is actually the query string itself. This can be retrieved and used (in this case equated with a new variable, called whichone) using Request.QueryString().

```
whichone = Request.QueryString("id")
```
The SQL command string can delete exactly those data in the table where EmployeeID has the same value as whichone.

```
DELETE FROM Employees WHERE EmployeeID = " & whichone
```
The SQL syntax is DELETE FROM table name WHERE criterion. With DELETE, one or several fields are deleted according to the WHERE criterion.

As in Example S, the second part of the script uses the Command object to execute the SQL in the database, because we do not need to see the data again (i.e., we do not need to make a Recordset). We just need to delete the existing information.

Example U: Updating a Database

In this example two ASP files are used first to select the person whose data should be updated and then to replace the data in certain fields, using the SQL UPDATE command. Notice the variables whichone, id, and EmployeeID and how they change between the two files. This underlines the importance of keeping a strict check on your variables, as well as the need to debug in a different file from the one you get the error report in.

1. Open your HTML editor and type the following:

```
<%@ Language=VBScript%>
<HTML>
<BODY>
<H1>Which person's data should be updated?</H1>
<%
Dim whichone, objRec
whichone = Request.QueryString("id")
Set objRec = Server.CreateObject ("ADODB.Recordset")
If whichone = "" Then
objRec.Open "SELECT EmployeeID,FirstName,LastName FROM Employees", _
"Driver={Microsoft Access Driver (*.MDB)}; DBQ=" & _
Server.MapPath("northwind.mdb")
Do While Not objRec.EOF
Response.Write "<A HREF='correct.asp?id=" & objRec("EmployeeID") _
& "'>" & objRec("FirstName") & " "
Response.Write objRec("LastName") & "</A><BR>"
objRec.MoveNext
Loop
Else
objRec.Open "SELECT * FROM Employees WHERE EmployeeID = " & _
whichone, "Driver={Microsoft Access Driver (*.MDB)}; DBQ=" & _
Server.MapPath("northwind.mdb")
Response.Write "<FORM ACTION='correctnow.asp' Method='get'><TABLE>"
Do While Not objRec.EOF
Response.Write "<TR><TD Colspan=2><INPUT TYPE='HIDDEN' VALUE='" _
& objRec("EmployeeID") & "' NAME='id'></TD></TR>"
Response.Write "<TR><TD>First Name:</TD><TD><INPUT TYPE='TEXT' _
VALUE='" & objRec("FirstName") & "' NAME='FirstName'></TD></TR>"
Response.Write "<TR><TD>Last Name:</TD><TD><INPUT TYPE='TEXT' _
```

```
           VALUE='" & objRec("LastName") & "' NAME='Lastname'></TD></TR>"
           Response.Write "<TR><TD>Title:</TD><TD><INPUT TYPE='TEXT' _
           VALUE='" & objRec("Title") & "' NAME='Title'></TD></TR>" _
           Response.Write "<TR><TD>Title of Courtesy:</TD><TD><INPUT TYPE='TEXT' _
           VALUE='" & objRec("TitleOfCourtesy") & "' NAME='TitleOfCourtesy'></TD></TR>"
           Response.Write "<TR><TD>Date of Birth:</TD><TD><INPUT TYPE='TEXT' VALUE='" & _
           objRec("BirthDate") & "' NAME='BirthDate'></TD></TR>" _
           Response.Write "<TR><TD>Employed Since:</TD><TD><INPUT TYPE='TEXT' VALUE='" & _
           objRec("HireDate") & "' NAME='HireDate'></TD></TR>"
           Response.Write "<TR><TD>Address:</TD><TD><INPUT TYPE='TEXT' VALUE='" & _
           objRec("Address") & "' NAME='Address'><BR>"
           Response.Write "<TR><TD>City:</TD><TD><INPUT TYPE='TEXT' VALUE='" & _
           objRec("City") & "' NAME='City'></TD></TR>"
           Response.Write "<TR><TD>Region:</TD><TD><INPUT TYPE='TEXT' VALUE='" & _
           objRec("Region") & "' NAME='Region'></TD></TR>"
           Response.Write "<TR><TD>Zip Code:</TD><TD><INPUT TYPE='TEXT' VALUE='" & _
           objRec("PostalCode") & "' NAME='PostalCode'></TD></TR>"_
           Response.Write "<TR><TD>Country:</TD><TD><INPUT TYPE='TEXT' VALUE='" & _
           objRec("Country") & "' NAME='Country'></TD></TR>"
           Response.Write "<TR><TD>Home Telephone:</TD><TD><INPUT TYPE='TEXT' VALUE='" & _
           objRec("HomePhone") & "' NAME='HomePhone'></TD></TR>"_
           Response.Write "<TR><TD>Telephone Extension:</TD><TD><INPUT TYPE='TEXT' _
           VALUE='" & objRec("Extension") & "' NAME='Extension'></TD></TR>"
           Response.Write "<TR><TD>Notes:</TD><TD><Textarea NAME='Notes'>" & _
           objRec("Notes") & "</textarea></TD></TR>"
           Response.Write "<TR><TD>Reports To (number):</TD><TD><INPUT TYPE='TEXT' _
           VALUE='" & objRec("ReportsTo") & "' NAME='ReportsTo'></TD></TR>"
           Response.Write "<TR><TD></TD><TD><INPUT TYPE='SUBMIT' _
           VALUE='Update'></TD></TR></TABLE>"
           objRec.MoveNext
           Loop
```

```
End If
objRec.Close
Set objRec = Nothing
%>
</BODY>
</HTML>
```

2. Save this document as C:\inetpub\wwwroot\correct.asp.

3. In your HTML editor type the following:

```
<%@ Language=VBScript%>
<HTML>
<BODY>
<%
whichone = Request.QueryString("id")
FirstName = Request.QueryString("FirstName")
LastName = Request.QueryString("LastName")
Title = Request.QueryString("Title")
TitleOfCourtesy = Request.QueryString("TitleOfCourtesy")
Birth = Request.QueryString("BirthDate")
Hire = Request.QueryString("HireDate")
Address = Request.QueryString("Address")
City = Request.QueryString("City")
Region = Request.QueryString("Region")
PostalCode = Request.QueryString("PostalCode")
Country = Request.QueryString("Country")
HomePhone = Request.QueryString("HomePhone")
Extension = Request.QueryString("Extension")
Notes = Request.QueryString("Notes")
Reports = Request.QueryString("ReportsTo")
'Birth Hire and Reports are now the wrong type
```

```
'of variable so they are converted as follows
BirthDate = CDate(Birth)
HireDate = CDate(Hire)
ReportsTo = CInt(Reports)
Dim strSql
strSql = "UPDATE Employees SET " &_
"FirstName='" & FirstName &_
"', LastName='" & Lastname &_
"', Title='" & Title &_
"', TitleOfCourtesy='" & TitleOfCourtesy &_
"', BirthDate='" & BirthDate &_
"', HireDate='" & HireDate &_
"', Address='" & Address &_
"', City='" & City &_
"', Region='" & Region &_
"', PostalCode='" & PostalCode &_
"', Country='" & Country &_
"', HomePhone='" & HomePhone &_
"', Extension='" & Extension &_
"', Notes='" & Notes &_
"', ReportsTo='" & ReportsTo & _
"' WHERE EmployeeID = " & whichone
Dim objCmd
Set objCmd = Server.CreateObject("ADODB.Command")
objCmd.ActiveConnection = "Driver={Microsoft Access Driver _
(*.MDB)}; DBQ=" & Server.MapPath("northwind.mdb")
objCmd.CommandText = strSql
objCmd.Execute
Set objCmd = Nothing
Response.Write "<H1>Many thanks ...</H1><BR>" & FirstName & _
" " & LastName & " has been updated<BR>"
```

```
%>
</BODY>
</HTML>
```

4. Save this document as C:\inetpub\wwwroot\correctnow.asp.

5. Open your browser and type **http://localhost/correct.asp** in the address field.

Explanation

As in Example T (delete.asp), the script in correct.asp is divided by an If/Else statement into two parts. EmployeeID is retrieved from the database and used in two ways, both in the If statement and in the SQL command string (if the variable whichone contains no value). The SQL string collects the EmployeeID, FirstName, and LastName of all data rows into one Recordset:

```
objRec.Open "SELECT EmployeeID,FirstName,LastName FROM
Employees",
```

Each person is now represented by a hyperlink, to which their EmployeeID is attached by means of a query string. When the link is clicked, the file correct.asp is reloaded (because the link returns to it). But this time the variable whichone is different from empty, meaning that the Else part of the script is executed. The Recordset is opened again, but this time only for the data in the row of the person you clicked on. Notice the use of WHERE.

```
objRec.Open "SELECT * FROM Employees WHERE EmployeeID = " & _
whichone
```

So now a series of input boxes are constructed whose values are the data from the Recordset (a slight exception is the <textarea> used for "Notes," as <textarea> does not have a value). This means that they can be corrected and submitted again. Notice that they are each assigned a name, which becomes the variable name in the next file. For simplicity, the same names are kept here.

```
Response.Write "<TR><TD>First Name:</TD><TD><INPUT TYPE='TEXT' _
VALUE='" & objRec("FirstName") & "' NAME='FirstName'></TD></TR>"
```

After correcting the data field values, the data can be submitted to the second file, correctnow.asp, by a click on the **Submit** button.

In correctnow.asp, the variables are collected using Request.QueryString. This method could not have been used if the FORM METHOD had been POST (in that case Request.Form would have had to be used), but here the FORM METHOD in correct.asp has been set to GET, which allows the use of Request.QueryString. The variables are converted to the correct type and then the database fields are equated to the correct variable values using the SQL string:

```
UPDATE Employees SET " & "FirstName='" & FirstName & _
"', LastName='" & LastName & _
"'
WHERE EmployeeID = " & whichone
```

The basic syntax is

```
UPDATE tablename SET column1=value,column2=value WHERE criterion
```

Notice that the column/value pairs are concatenated with a comma, but that a comma before WHEN will return an error.

Example V: Retrieving Data from Several Tables Using JOIN

In the previous example, we saw that ReportsTo returns a number. Clearly, it would be better to have the names attached to those numbers. One possibility would be to have a drop-down menu like

```
<select name="ReportsTo">
<option value="1">Buchanan, Steven</option>
<option value="2"> Callahan, Laura</option>
etc ...
</select>
```

However, it is also clear that it would be a good idea to be able to look at several tables simultaneously. The easiest way of doing this is to construct a Query in the database and use ASP to query that.

Unfortunately, Internet programmers are not always able to use the database as they wish, especially if it belongs to someone else (for example a travel bureau querying an airline company's time-table database). Therefore, the correct SQL has to be written in the programmers own ASP document.

1. Open your HTML editor and type the following:

```
<%@ Language=VBScript%>
<HTML>
<HEAD>
</HEAD>
<BODY>
<FORM ACTION="join.asp" METHOD="post">
<INPUT TYPE="TEXT" NAME="employee"><BR>
The input criterion is <B>Employee Last Name</B><BR>
<INPUT TYPE="SUBMIT" VALUE="Search">
</FORM><BR><BR>
<%
strEmployee=request.Form("employee")
Dim objRec
strConnect = "Driver={Microsoft Access Driver (*.MDB)}; _
DBQ="& Server.MapPath("northwind.mdb")
Set objRec = Server.CreateObject("ADODB.Recordset")
objRec.Open "SELECT * FROM Employees INNER JOIN Orders ON _
Employees.EmployeeID=Orders.EmployeeID WHERE _
Employees.LastName='" & strEmployee & _
"' ORDER BY Orders.ShipCountry", strConnect
Do While Not objRec.EOF
```

```
countup = countup + 1
objRec.MoveNext
Loop
If countup > 0 Then
Response.Write strEmployee & " has been responsible for " & _
countup & " orders </B><P>"
Response.write "The customers have been:<BR><BR>"
objRec.MoveFirst
Do While Not objRec.EOF
Response.Write "Firm: <B>" & objRec("ShipName") & ", in " _
& objRec("ShipCountry") & ", the " & objRec("OrderDate")
Response.Write "</B><HR Height='1' Width='250' align='left'>"
objRec.MoveNext
Loop
Else
Response.Write "Sorry, nothing found!<P>"
End If
objRec.Close
Set objRec = Nothing
%>
</BODY>
</HTML>
```

2. Save the document as C:\Inetpub\wwwroot\join.asp.

3. Start your browser and type **http://localhost/join.asp** in the address field.

4. Write one of the employee names (e.g., Davolio) in the input box and click **Search**.

Explanation

This example is very much like Example R, with the difference being in the SQL command string. For the sake of this explanation the SQL has been chopped up into its four parts (remember that in ASP, it has to be on one line):

```
"SELECT * FROM Employees INNER JOIN Orders
ON Employees.EmployeeID = Orders.EmployeeID
WHERE Employees.LastName='" & strEmployee & "'
ORDER BY Orders.ShipCountry
```

All are selected FROM the first table, Employees, where an INNER JOIN exists to the second table, Orders. Next, the exact join has to be specified using ON, and the column in the first table has to be equated with the corresponding column in the second table. Note the use of "dot syntax" here (tablename1.columnname1= tablename2.columnname2), as this is the only way that columns in database tables can be exactly specified.

WHERE and ORDER BY are two criteria. Notice that once the INNER JOIN has been established, then the different selection criteria can easily refer to two different tables. WHERE picks out the LastName of the person we want, and ORDER BY orders the data in alphabetical sequence (it would have been by counting if the data had been numerical).

Using AND, various other criteria could have been added after WHERE; for example, AND Orders.Freight > 50 to get rid of small orders. The interested programmer can read some further common SQL commands later.

Notice that when we come to Response.Write, we use objRec("ShipName") and not the dot syntax objRec("Orders.ShipName"). This is because we are referring to the object Recordset table we constructed and are no longer referring to the database tables.

Example W: How to Find Out How Many
Rows Are in a Database—Returning Variables

1. Open your HTML editor and type the following:

```
<%@ Language=VBScript%>
<HTML>
<HEAD>
</HEAD>
<BODY>
<H1>How many rows does a database table have?</H1>
<%
strConnect = "Driver={Microsoft Access Driver (*.MDB)}; _
DBQ=" & Server.MapPath("northwind.mdb")
Set objForb = Server.CreateObject("ADODB.connection")
objInvestigate.Open strConnect
Set objRec = objForb.Execute("SELECT COUNT(Supplier) AS _
howmany FROM Products")
Response.Write objRec("howmany")
objInvestigate.Close
Set objForb = Nothing
%>
</BODY>
</HTML>
```

2. Save the document as C:\inetpub\wwwroot\count.asp.

3. Start your browser and type **http://localhost/count.asp** in the address field.

Explanation
The ADO object connection represents the "physical" connection to the database. It can be used to have several connections open simultaneously; for example, to several

databases. Here it is used to count up the number of rows in a table without reading the data. The SQL string is executed by means of the connection object and the resulting information stored in a Recordset.

```
Set objRec = objForb.Execute("SELECT COUNT(Supplier) AS howmany
FROM Products")
```

The syntax is SELECT COUNT(columnname) AS variable FROM tablename.

The command COUNT counts up the number of rows in the named column. Which column is irrelevant, as all columns are the same length. Then it returns the result as a variable. In "reality" this represents a new field in the Recordset. The actual data is retrieved using

```
Response.Write objRec("howmany")
```

as if "howmany" were a column name. After writing the field, the connection is closed and the object is eliminated from memory.

A REVIEW OF SQL

Table 7: Some useful commands in SQL

Command	Result
SELECT * FROM tablename	Retrieves all data from the table.
SELECT column1,column2,column3 FROM tablename ORDER BY column3	Retrieves the named columns from the named table and sorts the data according to column3 (alphabetical or numerical). The order can be DESC (descending) or ASC (ascending), depending on how the data should be sorted. ASC is the default (it starts with the number 0 and works up). DESC starts at the highest number. When used, it is

Command	Result *(continued)*
	simply added to the end of the string, like SELECT column1,column2,column3 FROM tablename ORDER BY column3 DESC.
SELECT columnname1,columnname2, columnname3 FROM tablename WHERE columnname1='variable1' AND columnname2='variable2'	Retrieves the named columns from the named table and searches the rows in the columns named in WHERE for data matching the named variables. Only data fulfilling both criteria are returned. Both WHERE and AND, as well as OR, can be combined with NOT.
SELECT columnname1,columnname2, columnname3 FROM tablename WHERE columnname1='variable1' OR columnname2='variable2'	Retrieves the named columns from the named table and searches the rows in the columns named in WHERE for data matching the named variables. Data fulfilling both the first criterion as well as those fulfilling the second criterion are returned.
SELECT columnname1,columnname2 FROM tablename WHERE columnname1 LIKE '%variable%'	Retrieves the data in the named columns and searches for fields where the variable value is found anywhere. For example "U" will return positive for USA, Katmandu, Australia, and so on.
DELETE FROM tablename WHERE columnname LIKE 'variable'	Retrieves the data in the named column, searches the rows in the named column for fields where the variable value is, and deletes that whole row.

INSERT INTO tablename (column1,column2, column3) VALUES ('variable1','variable2', 'variable3')	Results in a whole new row being inserted into the named table, where the values of the variables are set into the columns. (The variable sequence and column sequence must correspond.)
UPDATE tablename SET column1 = 'variable1', column2 ='variable2' WHERE column3 = 'variable3'	Searches column3 for a row containing the value of variable3, then inserts the values of the other variables in the corresponding columns of that row, leaving other data untouched.
SELECT * FROM tablename1 INNER JOIN tablename2 ON tablename1.joinedcolumn= tablename2.joinedcolumn WHERE tablename.anycolumn = 'variable'	Retrieves all data from both tables where any column (anycolumn, which can be in either of the tables) contains the value of the variable.
SELECT * FROM tablename WHERE column1 BETWEEN variablelownumber AND variablehighnumber	Returns all data from the named table where the numerical values (not text!) in the named column are between the values contained in the variables. This is similar to WHERE column1 >=variable1 AND column1 <= variable2. Notice in the latter case the column name is specified twice.
SELECT DISTINCT columnname FROM tablename	Returns all the data in the named column in the named table but excludes doubled data. That is, if Saturday were found several times, it would be found only once in the Recordset.
SELECT COUNT(columnname) AS variable FROM tablename	Counts the number of rows in the named column and returns that value as a variable.

THE LOG FILE OBJECT

It can be very useful to find out who has been visiting your Web site, how often, etc. This data is stored on the server and can be retrieved very easily. The next two examples look at how to do this. Before trying the next two examples, check that you do not have any files called log.txt or counter.log in C:\inetpub\wwwroot.

Example X: Visitor Data—Who Are They and What Platform Are They Using?

1. Open your HTML editor and type the following:

```
<%
'ForAppending = 8, ForReading = 1, ForWriting = 2
Dim strLogFileName
strLogFileName=Server.MapPath("log.txt")
dim objFSO
set objFSO = CreateObject("Scripting.FileSystemObject")
Dim myFile
If objFSO.FileExists(strLogFileName) Then
Set myFile=objFSO.OpenTextFile(strLogFileName, 8)
Else
Set myFile=objFSO.CreateTextFile(strLogFileName)
End If
myFile.WriteLine "Date: " & Date & " Time: " & Time
myFile.WriteLine "IP:" & Request.ServerVariables("LOCAL_ADDR")
myFile.WriteLine "Browser:" & _
Request.ServerVariables("HTTP_USER_AGENT")
myFile.Close
Set objFSO = Nothing
%>
```

```
Ok... <%=strLogFileName%>  from IP:
<%=Request.ServerVariables("LOCAL_ADDR")%>
```

2. Save the document as C:\inetpub\wwwroot\logfile.asp.

3. Start your browser and type **http://localhost/logfile.asp** in the address field.

4. Find and open C:\inetpub\wwwroot\log.txt.

Explanation

First a new variable is declared whose value is the server's path to the file we wish to use to record data:

```
strLogFileName=Server.MapPath("log.txt")
```

This is followed by a second new variable containing the command to create a new object:

```
set objFSO = CreateObject("Scripting.FileSystemObject")
```

Scripting objects are objects that can be used in any form of script, either server- or client-side (in contrast to ASP objects, which are only server-side). The FileSystemObject allows access to all the files stored on the server. Thus, with

```
If objFSO.FileExists(strLogFileName) Then
Set myFile=objFSO.OpenTextFile(strLogFileName, 8)
```

we can test if a file exists with the location and name specified in srtLogFileName, (if yes) open it with OpenTextFile, and set it to the default-specified value of 8, which stands for "for appending" (so we can add text after already existing text). If you have NT4 with the help files installed, then you can read more about OpenTextFile at **http://localhost/iishelp/vbscript/htm/vbs352.htm**.

If the text file does not already exist, then we can create it (at the required location). Check C:\inetpub\wwwroot again to see if log.txt exists.

```
Else
Set myFile=objFSO.CreateTextFile(strLogFileName)
```

Now we know either the file exists and is opened or it has just been created. Therefore we can write to it:

```
myFile.WriteLine "Date: " & Date & " Time: " & Time
myFile.WriteLine "IP:" & Request.ServerVariables("LOCAL_ADDR")
myFile.WriteLine "Browser:" &
Request.ServerVariables("HTTP_USER_AGENT")
```

After this the connection is closed and the object eliminated:

```
myFile.Close
Set objFSO = Nothing
```

The new contents of log.txt should then look something like

```
Date: 30-02-00 Time: 14:09:46
IP:127.0.0.1
Browser:Mozilla/4.0 (compatible; MSIE 5.0; Windows 98; DigExt)
```

where Date and Time are the standard functions we saw in Example A. LOCAL_ADDR is the IP number of the PC. On an open Web site it may be preferable to use REMOTE_ADDR, which records the IP number of the Internet service provider.

HTTP_USER_AGENT returns details of the browser used and the platform. These can be used in, for example, building a browser check referring visitors to browser-specific pages.

Finally, the HTML and inline code

```
Ok... <%=strLogFileName%>  from IP:
<%=Request.ServerVariables("LOCAL_ADDR")%>
```

should show a browser window something like

```
Ok... C:\inetpub\wwwroot\log.txt from IP: 127.0.0.1
```

Notice that although strLogFileName was originally only defined to Server.MapPath("log.txt"), the server returns an absolute path in the PC. As above, LOCAL_ADDR returns the PC's default IP number.

Example Y: A Visitor Counter (An Introduction to Constants)

This example introduces the concepts of constants. Constants are similar to variables. But whereas a variable's value may change during the course of executing a script, the value of a constant cannot. Defining constants overrides the default values.

1. Open your HTML editor and type the following:

```
<%
Const ForAppending = 8, ForReading = 1, ForWriting = 2
dim strLogFileName
strLogFileName = Server.MapPath("counter.log")
Response.Write "<table width='100%'><TR><TD bgcolor='navy'
colspan='2'>  </TD></TR>"
Response.Write "<TR><TD bgcolor='gold'>We are writing to:
</TD><TD bgcolor='yellow'> " & strLogFileName & "</TD><BR>"
Response.Write "<table width='100%'><TR><TD bgcolor='navy'
colspan='2'>  </TD></TR>"
Dim intCount
intCount = 1
myFile = TextStream
'text files should be text stream by default
'but it is better to be sure
Dim objFSO
Set objFSO = CreateObject("Scripting.FileSystemObject")
If objFSO.FileExists(strLogFileName) Then
Set myFile = objFSO.OpenTextFile(strLogFileName)
intCount = myFile.ReadAll
```

```
'here we get the counts in case of previous hits
intCount = intCount + 1
End If
Response.Write "<table width='100%'><TR><TD bgcolor='navy'
colspan='2'>  </TD></TR>"
Response.Write "<TR><TD bgcolor='gold'>There have been:
</TD><TD bgcolor='yellow'> " & intCount & " hits</TD><BR>"
Response.Write "<table width='100%'><TR><TD bgcolor='navy'
colspan='2'>  </TD></TR>"
If objFSO.FileExists(strLogFileName) Then
Set myFile=objFSO.OpenTextFile(strLogFileName, ForWriting)
Else
Set myFile=objFSO.CreateTextFile(strLogFileName)
End If
myFile.WriteLine intCount
'here we write intCount
myFile.Close
Set objFSO = Nothing
%>
```

2. Save the document as C:\inetpub\wwwroot\visitcounter.asp.

3. Start your browser and type **http://localhost/visitcounter.asp** in the address field.

4. Refresh your browser several times.

Explanation

Again here the FileScriptingObject and its object TextStream are used. The FileSystemObject has two methods: CreateTextFile and OpenTextFile. In this example (as in Example X) an If/Else statement checks if the file we wish to write to exists and, if not, creates it.

The TextStream object methods encompass Close, Read, ReadAll, ReadLine, Skip, SkipLine, Write, WriteLine (used here and also in Example X), and WriteBlankLines.

```
intCount = myFile.ReadAll
```

For each hit (when counter.log is opened) the variable intCount is incremented by one

```
intCount=intCount + 1
```

and the result written to counter.log. Because the file is opened "ForWriting," the previous value is over-written (compare this with Example X, where log.txt was opened "ForAppending") and the result is seen using WriteLine.

If you have NT4 installed with help files, you can read more about the ReadAll method at **http://localhost/iishelp/vbscript/htm/vbs360.htm**.

PROCEDURES

Procedures are pieces of code resulting in a certain event happening. VBScript contains several built-in examples of this, but it is also possible to define custom Procedures. VBScript contains two forms of Procedures, called Subprocedures and Functions. The difference between Functions and Subprocedures is that Functions are executed to return a new value, while Subprocedures simply execute code. These two types can be global or local. Global Procedures are defined in global.asa (see page 51), so here purely local examples are given. These are normally defined at the beginning of a file and can be called from any point in the following code.

Functions are defined within Function and End Function. Subprocedures are defined within Sub and End Sub. Functions are called using functionname(arguments). Subprocedures are called using Call subname(arguments). If no arguments are to be used, then empty parentheses are used.

FUNCTIONS

An example of a built-in Function is

```
nine=CStr(9)
```

This standard Function called "CStr" sets the value of the variable called "nine" to be a text string containing the character 9.

When you define a Function yourself, it may look like

```
Function PrintOutMsg(msg,count)
Dim i
For i = 1 to count
Response.Write(msg & "<BR>")
Next
PrintOutMsg=count
End Function
```

At any appropriate point in the following document this Function can be called using the arguments specified.

```
<%
Dim x
x=PrintOutMsg("this is a function test",4)
'this calls the Function, provides the arguments,
'and returns a value for x
Response.Write "<P> the message has been printed " & x & " times"
%>
```

SUBPROCEDURES

In a parallel fashion, we can make our own Subprocedures.

```
Sub PrintOutMsg(msg,count)
Dim i
For i = 1 to count
Response.Write(msg & "<BR>")
Next
End Sub
```

This Subprocedure can be called at a later point using

```
<%
Call PrintOutMsg("this is a sub test",4)
%>
```

Example Z: Using Procedures

In Examples X and Y, HTML formatting was added. This adds a lot of code and small errors can always creep in. In the following example Subprocedures are used to add the "life" to a page in an easy and convenient way.

1. Open your HTML editor and type the following:

```
<HTML>
<HEAD>
<%
Dim intLastRecord, rows, strCaption
intLastRecord = 20
'intLastRecord is the number of products to be shown
rows = intLastRecord + 2
'rows is the row-span of the side columns
'Since the top table takes up 2 rows they must be 2 longer than
'the database results
strCaption = "Our " & intLastRecord & " Most Popular Products"
Sub Table1()
Response.Write "<P align='center'><table width='100%'></TR>"
Response.Write "<TD colspan='3' align='center'><FONT SIZE='4' COLOR='black'
face='arial'>"  & strCaption & "</FONT></TD></TR>"
Response.Write "<TR><TD bgcolor='navy' align='center'
width='62%'><font color='white'> Product Name </font></TD>"
Response.Write "<TD bgcolor='navy' align='center'><font color='white'>
Price </font></TD>"
Response.Write "<TD bgcolor='navy' align='center'><font color='white'>
Re-order Level </font></TD></TR>"
Response.Write "</TR></table></P>"
End Sub
Sub Table2()
Response.Write "<TD BGCOLOR='gray' width='50' rowspan='" & _
rows & "'>  <BR></TD>"
End Sub
%>
</HEAD>
<BODY bgcolor="white">
<%
```

```
'start the HTML layout
Response.Write "<DIV ALIGN='center'><TABLE WIDTH='100%' _
CELLSPACING='10' CELLPADDING='0' border='0'><TR>"
'write the first flanking column
Call Table2()
'write the first table
Response.Write "<TD colspan='3'>"
Call Table1()
Response.Write "</TD>"
'write the second flanking column
Call Table2()
response.Write "</TR>"
strCon = "Driver={Microsoft Access Driver (*.mdb)}; DBQ=" & _
Server.MapPath("northwind.mdb")
Set rsProd = Server.CreateObject("ADODB.Recordset")
rsProd.Open "SELECT * FROM Products ORDER BY ReorderLevel DESC", strCon
'test if anything exists
If (rsProd.BOF AND rsProd.EOF) Then
Response.Write "Sorry, no products found."
Else
intRowNumber = 0
Do Until rsProd.EOF OR intRowNumber = intLastRecord
'using mod we see if a row number is even or odd, and
'give different cell background colors
intRowNumber = intRowNumber + 1
If (intRowNumber Mod 2) = 0 Then
strBGColor = "silver"
Else
strBGColor = "cornflowerblue"
End If
'write the results
```

```
Response.Write "<TR>" _
    & "<TD BGCOLOR='" & strBGColor & "' ALIGN='left' width='55%'>" _
    & "<B>" & rsProd("Product Name") & "</B>" _
    & "</TD>" _
    & "<TD BGCOLOR='" & strBGColor & "' ALIGN='center'>" _
    & rsProd("Unit Price") & "</TD>" _
    & "<TD BGCOLOR='" & strBGColor & "' ALIGN='left'>" _
    & rsProd("ReorderLevel") & "</TR>"
rsProd.MoveNext
Loop
End If
rsProd.Close
Set rsProd = Nothing
%>
</TABLE></DIV>
</BODY>
</HTML>
```

2. Save the document as C:\inetpub\wwwroot\product.asp.

3. Open you browser and type **http://localhost/product.asp** in the address field.

Explanation

The variable intLastRecord is set to how many results are to be shown. This is both set into the caption variable

```
strCaption = "Our " & intLastRecord & " Most Popular Products"
```

and also used in searching the database

```
Do Until rsProd.EOF OR intRowNumber = intLastRecord
```

HTML layout information is given in three places: in two Subprocedures and inline using Response.Write. Upon loading the body, these are called (for example `Call Table2()`) in the order we wish to have the layout.

The SQL string selects all the data and orders it according to popularity; i.e., ORDER BY the column ReorderLevel in reverse order (DESC), so that those with a high number are shown first. At this point an If/Else statement checks that something matching the criteria is in the database:

```
If (rsProd.BOF AND rsProd.EOF) Then
```

If both beginning of file and end of file are false, then the If is true; i.e., nothing has been found. Otherwise a new variable intRowNumber is defined, set to 0, and incremented by one for each loop:

```
intRowNumber = intRowNumber + 1
```

A simple If/Else statement checks if this is an even-numbered row or an odd-numbered row and sets the value of a new variable accordingly:

```
If (intRowNumber Mod 2) = 0 Then
strBGColor = "silver"
```

and the new variable is set in the Response.Write HTML in the results part of the table:

```
"<TD BGCOLOR='" & strBGColor & "'
```

Home Exercise 3 (this should take you a whole weekend)

The point of this exercise is to make a Web site for two quite different types of users, Customers and Administrators, such that Customers can see and order all the firm's products, and the Administrators can log on, add and delete products, and see Customers' orders.

Use at least a weekend on this exercise. If you don't have time to do it all, then read it first and concentrate on the bits of functionality (not layout) that interest you.

Images

If you wish to show images, remember that ASP and Access make a bad combination in terms of pictures (images) and preformatted hyperlinks. To show the pictures of the products, remove the images (bitmap fragments) from the database. Save them separately in a subdirectory, with the image names corresponding to their row number (e.g., if the catagory number is 1, then the file is saved as images/1.jpg). Show the images in the ASP file using inline coding. For example,

```
<img src="<% objRec("catagory number") %>.jpg">
```

Customers

A customer starts at index.asp. Here the catagories of products (table "Categories"), together with short descriptions, can be seen. By clicking on a catagory, the customer comes to another side where they can see a complete list of the products (and relevant details, like price, weight, and producer) in that catagory (table "Products"). It is a good idea to have the layout subprocedures ready, perhaps contained in .inc files. The customer may order a product by clicking on it. Here a new side opens, and the product number is taken over using a hidden field. The customer details have to be typed in (for required fields, see table "Orders"). When the customer clicks "Submit," the table is updated with that customer's order and date.

Can you think of how customers could order several products at once? How can you check that a product is available? What should happen if it is not available?

A "Submit Tip"

If input type="submit" is used, a gray button appears. If you want to use an image instead, use

```
<input border="0" height="" width="" src="images/name.jpg"
type="image" value="submit" name="submit">
```

Administrators

Administrators are the people working at the firm. They can be found in the table "Coworkers." They open their part of the Web site at admin.htm, where they log in using their first name as their ID and their last name as their password. If the data input is correct, then the administrator is redirected to a file where they have two choices. They can click either to see a list of all products to update them or to see a list of all orders.

The list of products ends with a form. This form can be used to insert new products in the table "Products." Conversely, by a click on an already-existing product, the data can be accessed and individual fields updated.

The file with the list of all orders can have a bit too much information, especially if you choose to show all fields (you can also just show part of the order, e.g. number and date, and require an additional click to show the full details for that one order). Therefore, on this side there should be two tables. The first should show only the latest 10 orders, ordered by date. However, if there is lots of activity on the site, the latest 10 may not be sufficient to catch all the new orders. In this case a list of all orders may be needed too.

Is there a smarter way to see just those orders that are new and have not yet been filled? How about showing those orders that lack a coworker's name (in the third column)? This would be based on having the administrators update this line with their name when they fill an order. In fact, how about using hidden fields (or a cookie) to take this data over from the log-on side (admin.htm) and give the administrators a button to click when they have filled the order?

APPENDIX A

EXTENDING ASP OVER THE BORDERS
OF INTERNET INFORMATION SERVER

As explained in the section Software Compatibility, two Microsoft technologies, IIS and VBScript, form the basis of the ASP explained in this book. Although the Unix technologies are losing ground (not only to Microsoft), the various Unix "flavors" like Apache are probably still the most common server software. However, all Web servers support Internet Server API (ISAPI) extensions; thus various add-ons are available. These include those from Chilli!Soft as well as the open-source Apache::ASP, which uses a development of Perl called PerlScript.

Independent of which solution appeals to you, system format differences mean that the code still has to be translated to the supported language. In particular, one should pay attention to

- File names (length, spaces, length of extension)
- Paths (slash or backslash)
- Date and time code
- Data validation code
- Variable naming conventions (upper/lower cases, case sensitivity, reserved words)
- Standard function formats

APPENDIX B

THE OBJECT MODEL

This appendix covers the objects Request, Response, Application, Session, and Server.
Objects can have

- **Collections** In a Collection each piece of information is in a name/value pair. This is especially useful because data values are accessible simply by referring to their names.

- **Properties** Properties are static expressions that describe an object using an equals sign (e.g., name="Fred").

- **Methods** Methods do something active to the object, normally involving the attached data (e.g., Write).

- **Events** An Event is a signal responding when something happens. An Event can also start new events (e.g., OnClick).

Figure 5: A graphical overview

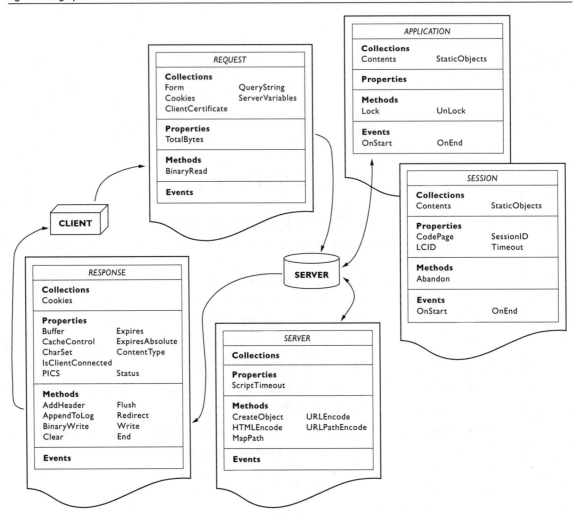

THE REQUEST OBJECT

Collection

Form	Collects form fields and sends the contents of these to the browser. **Syntax:** ``` For Each Item In Request.Form Response.Write "<P>" & item & " = " & Request.Form(item) Next ```
Cookies	Collects cookie fields and sends the contents of these to the browser. **Syntax:** ``` For Each Item In Request.Cookies Response.Write "<P>" & item & " = " & Request.Cookies(item) Next ```
ClientCertificate	Collects certificate values sent from the browser.
QueryString	**Syntax:** ``` For Each Item In Request.QueryString Response.Write "<P>" & item & " = " _ & Request.QueryString(item) Next ```
Server Variables	Collects server and HTTP variables.

Syntax:

```
For Each Item In Request.ServerVariables
Response.Write "<P>" & item & " = " & _
Request.ServerVariables(item)
Next
```

Properties

TotalBytes	TotalBytes contains the number of bytes sent to the client. This is a read-only property.

Methods

BinaryRead	The BinaryRead method is used to receive the data sent to the server as part of the POST request. **Syntax:** `Request.BinaryRead(variable)`

THE RESPONSE OBJECT

Collection

Cookies	Collects cookies sent to the browser. **Syntax:** `Response.Cookies(cookie)[(key)|.attribute] = value`

Properties

Buffer	**Syntax:** `Response.Buffer = True / False`

Methods

Clear	The Clear method deletes information in the buffer. **Syntax:** `Response.Clear`
End	The End method stops sending information to the browser. **Syntax:** `Response.End`
Flush	The Flush method sends information from the buffer to the browser. **Syntax:** `Response.Flush`
Redirect	The Redirect method shifts the browser from one side to another. **Syntax:** `Response.Redirect "newpage.htm/asp"`
Write	The Write method sends a specific string to the browser.

Syntax:

```
Response.Write "text"
```

THE APPLICATION OBJECT

Methods

Lock	The Lock method locks applications so others cannot change the applications' properties.

	Syntax:
	`Application.Lock`
	`Application("numberofUsers") =`
	`Application("numberofUsers "" + 1`

UnLock	UnLock removes a Lock. **Syntax:** `Application.UnLock`

Events

Session_OnStart	OnStart specifies what happens when an application starts.
Session_OnEnd	OnEnd specifies what happens when an application finishes.

STRING CONSTANTS

Constant	Value	Description
vbCr	Chr(13)	Carriage return only.
vbCrlf	Chr(13) & Chr(10)	Carriage return and line feed.
vbLf	Chr(10)	Line feed only.
vbNewLine	—	Newline character as appropriate to a specific platform.
vbNullChar	Chr(0)	Character having the value 0.
vbNullString	—	String having the value zero (not just an empty string).
vbTab	Chr(9)	Horizontal tab.

String constants are useful when you are setting up the structure of the code to be executed.

STRING FUNCTIONS

Function	Description
FormatCurrency	Returns a string formatted as currency.
FormatDateTime	Returns a string formatted as date or time.
FormatNumber	Returns a string formatted as a number.
FormatPercent	Returns a string formatted as a percentage.
InStr	Returns the position of the first occurrence of a given string in another string.

InstrRev	Returns the same as InStr, but beginning from the other end.
Join	Returns the content of a string resulting from the concatenation of strings in an array.
LCase	Returns a string where the characters are converted to lower case.
Left	Returns a specified number of characters (starting from the left) in a string.
Len	Returns the length of a string.
LTrim	Returns a copy of the content of a string without initial spaces.
Mid	Returns a given number of characters from a string.
Replace	Returns a string where a given part has been replaced a given number of times.
Right	Returns a given number of characters in a string, starting from the right.
RTrim	Returns a copy of a string without subsequent spaces.
Space	Returns a string containing a given number of spaces.
Split	Returns a one-dimensional array of a given number of strings.
StrComp	Returns a value with the result of a comparison between strings.

StrReverse	Returns a string where a series of characters have been inverted.
Trim	Returns a copy of a string where preceding and subsequent spaces have been removed.
UCase	Returns a string where characters have been converted to upper case.

DATE/TIME FUNCTIONS

Function	Description
Date	Returns the current date.
DateAdd	Returns the current date plus a given interval.
DateDiff	Returns the days, weeks, or years between two dates.
DatePart	Returns either the days, months, or years before a given date.
Day	Returns a number between 1 and 31 corresponding to the date at the server.
Hour	Returns the time (in hours) as a number between 0 and 23.
Minute	Returns the time (in minutes) as a number between 0 and 59.
Month	Returns the time (in months) as a number between 1 and 12.
MonthName	Returns the name of the current month as a text string.
Now	Returns the current date and time at the server.
Second	Returns a number between 0 and 59 corresponding to the current second.

Time	Returns a variant of Date with the current time (in hours).
TimeSerial	Returns a variant of Date (as Time) including hours, minutes, and seconds.
WeekDay	Returns a number corresponding to the current day of the week.
WeekdayName	Returns the name of a given week day as text string.
Year	Returns a number corresponding to the current year.

FURTHER INFORMATION ON THE INTERNET

Standard Sources
http://msdn.microsoft.com
http://www.activeserverpages.com
http://www.15seconds.com
http://www.asphole.com
http://www.asp101.com
http://www.aspalliance.com
http://www.4guysfromrolla.com
http://www.kamath.com/

Other Interesting Sites
(but who knows how long they'll be around)

| ASPSamples.com | Contains a collection of tutorials with sample ASP code. The code can be modified and tested online to see the effects immediately. |
| | **www.aspsamples.com** |

ASPcode	ASP code samples free for use. Additional code can be requested or submitted. **www.aspcode.com**
BorderStat Online Sample Scripts	Contains a few sample ASP scripts that can be downloaded and used on Web sites. **www.borderstat.com/freewebservice**
ASPCode.net	Offers free ASP scripts and code samples, categorized by topic for easy browsing. **www.aspcode.net**
CodeAve.com / ASP	Contains code samples showing various methods of programming Active Server Pages. Topics include hit counters, text file display, databases, random events, and others. **www.codeave.com/asp**
The ASP Emporium	Comprehensive collection of free ASP scripts and applications, free for use. **www.aspemporium.com/aspEmporium/index.asp**
15 Seconds	Code samples and tricks and tips on how to use Internet Information Server and Active Server Pages. Most of the samples include source code. **www.15seconds.com**

INDEX